The Andrew R. Cecil Lectures on Moral Values in a Free Society

established by

The University of Texas at Dallas

Volume VI

OUR FREEDOMS: RIGHTS AND RESPONSIBILITIES

Our Freedoms: Rights and Responsibilities

JERRE S. WILLIAMS
MAX L. STACKHOUSE
ARVO VAN ALSTYNE
ANDREW R. CECIL
RAY MARSHALL
EUGENE V. ROSTOW

With an Introduction by
ANDREW R. CECIL

Edited by
W. LAWSON TAITTE
The University of Texas at Dallas
1985

Library of Congress Catalog Card Number 85-050475
International Standard Book Number 0-292-76030-2

Distributed by the University of Texas Press,
Box 7819, Austin, Texas 78712

FOREWORD

The Andrew R. Cecil Lectures on Moral Values in a Free Society have become a valued tradition at The University of Texas at Dallas since they were established in 1979. The week of November 12, 1984, marked the sixth annual series in this continuing program. Each year scholars and leaders of national prominence share with the academic community and the public their most carefully considered reflections concerning the moral values that our country was built on. The program offers a unique opportunity for analysis and debate of the moral basis of a free society. In providing this forum, the University is fulfilling its responsibility to see that these values are understood and preserved.

The lectures are named for Dr. Andrew R. Cecil, the University's Distinguished Scholar in Residence and the Chancellor Emeritus of The Southwestern Legal Foundation. As President of the Foundation, his leadership of that institution gained him the highest respect in educational and legal circles throughout the United States. When he became Chancellor Emeritus of the Foundation, Dr. Cecil consented to serve as Distinguished Scholar in Residence at The University of Texas at Dallas. The Lectures on Moral Values in a Free Society are aptly named for a man who, throughout his career, has consistently been concerned with the moral verities, always stressing a faith in the dignity and worth of every individual.

The 1984 lectures were organized around the theme "Our Freedoms: Rights and Responsibilities." The five persons who joined Dr. Cecil all have contributed to learning and knowledge through distinguished academic careers in addition to serving our society in other important ways: as jurist, as theologian and pastor, as Commissioner of higher education, as former Cabinet member, as public servant. All of these scholars have, in offering so much of themselves in public service, demonstrated a profound grasp of the responsibility required in preserving our freedoms. We are most grateful to Messrs. Williams, Stackhouse, Van Alstyne, Cecil, Marshall, and Rostow for their willingness to share their ideas and for the thoughtful lectures that are preserved in this volume.

U.T. Dallas also wishes to extend its appreciation to all those who have helped make the lectures an important part of the life of the University, especially to the supporters of the Cecil Lectures. Through their contributions these donors enable us to continue this important educational endeavor and to publish the proceedings of the lectures, thus ensuring a wide and permanent audience for the ideas they present.

I am confident that all those who read the lectures published in the sixth volume of the Andrew R. Cecil Lectures on Moral Values in a Free Society, *Our Freedoms: Rights and Responsibilities*, will be stimulated to give additional thought to the vital issues discussed.

ROBERT H. RUTFORD, President
The University of Texas at Dallas
January, 1985

CONTENTS

INTRODUCTION

by

Andrew R. Cecil

Freedom is a state of mind subject to the inexorable laws of growth and decay. It is a concept, an ideal shared by civilized people everywhere. It is a positive force, and its essential exponents are free people. In his "Speech on Moving His Resolutions for Conciliation with the Colonies" delivered on March 22, 1775, Edmund Burke remarked, "In the character of the Americans a love of freedom is the predominating feature which marks and distinguishes the whole." Our civil, constitutional, and human rights are our birthright as citizens. The government or our fellow citizens cannot deny or abridge them, and they can be limited only under carefully defined conditions. Because of the strength of this love of freedom, our nation was endowed with a sense of mission expressed in the opening paragraph of the *Federalist* papers. By our "conduct and example," our people hoped to demonstrate to all the world the advantages of a free and self-governing society. The fulfillment of this mission became known as the "Great American Experiment" based on faith in self-government and belief in human dignity.

Wrote Madison, "We rest all our political experiments on mankind's capacity for self-government." The conception of a free self-governing society has, according to Jefferson, three main features: first, freely given or uncoerced consent; second, the principle of majority rule—*lex majoris partis*—which is "the fundamental law of every society of individuals of equal rights"; and third, the right to dissent, on which right are based the freedoms of speech, press, and peaceable assembly and all the other freedoms derived from them. These three features offer the means to prevent the absorption of all powers by the government and to protect the individual against the possible tyranny of his government.

The people, observed Jefferson, are "the only safe depositories" because American colonies were founded upon the premise that nothing is more valuable than the individual's worth and dignity, which is derived from man's unique relationship to the Creator of the Universe. This faith in the individual's "greatness" was expressed beautifully by Walt Whitman:

> "I swear I begin to see the meaning of these things!
> . . . it is not America who is so great,
> It is not I who am great, or to be great—it is you up
>   there, or anyone;
> It is to walk rapidly through civilizations, gov-
>   ernments, theories,
> Through poems, pageants, shows, to form great
>   individuals.
> Underneath all, individuals! . . .
> The American compact is altogether with in-
>   dividuals . . ."

Freedom is not static. It is a spark with magnetic powers of attraction. It has attracted more than three million Germans, who have gone from East to West; more than 200,000 Hungarians, who escaped to freedom during the rebellion in 1956; and hundreds of thousands of Vietnamese, Cambodians, and Laotians, who left their countries behind and took the risk of being killed and raped by modern-day pirates and marauders. Escaping from deception, coercion, terrorism, and assassination, they left their homeland, friends, families, and possessions. The pain and desperation that forced their escape can only be compared to the suffering of an animal that, in order to escape from captivity, gnaws off its own limb when that limb is constrained in a trap.

The government can discharge its responsibilities for the welfare of the nation and of the individual without depriving the people of their right to participate freely in the formulation of laws and without the danger of dictatorship and tyranny. To avoid such danger and to preserve the democratic state, it is imperative for the individual to preserve his sense of responsibility for the integrity of the government. Thomas Paine wrote, "Those who expect to reap the blessings of freedom must, like men, undergo the fatigue of supporting it." The price of freedom is eternal vigilance on the part of the citizen and his participation, whenever an adequate opportunity arises, in the function of government. The first ten amendments to the Constitution were added to preserve the precarious balance between liberty as self-government and liberty as the freedom of the individual from government.

Within that framework came freedom of peaceable assembly; the right to keep and bear arms; the pro-

hibition of peacetime quartering of troops without
consent; the prohibition of more than one punishment
or one trial for the same offense (double jeopardy);
protection against self-incrimination (no person can be
compelled to witness against himself); protection
against loss of life, liberty, or property without due
process of law; freedom from excessive bail and from
unreasonable searches and seizures; and the right to
speedy and public trial. The Constitution and the Bill
of Rights assert the existence of certain liberties of the
American citizen that are a part of our government.
Are these great documents the source of our freedom?
Learned Hand, the illustrious judge, once wrote: "I
often wonder whether we do not rest our hopes too
much upon constitutions, upon laws and upon courts.
These are false hopes, believe me, these are false
hopes. Liberty lies in the hearts of men and women;
when it dies there, no constitution, no law, no court
can even do much to help it. While it is there, it needs
no constitution, no law, no court to save it." (Learned
Hand, "Speech to Newly Naturalized Citizens, May
21, 1944," *The Spirit of Liberty*, Irving Dilliard, Ed.,
Alfred A. Knopf, Inc., 1952, p. 189.)

In the same spirit, Martin Luther long before
observed that "There can be no better instructions in
. . . all transactions in temporal goods than that every
man who is to deal with his neighbor present to himself these commandments: 'What ye would that others
should do unto you, do ye also unto them,' and 'love
thy neighbor as thyself.' If these were followed out,
then everything would instruct and arrange itself; then
no law books nor courts nor judicial actions would be
required; all things would quietly and simply be set to

rights, for everyone's heart and conscience would guide him."

The Declaration of Independence, the Constitution of the United States, and the Bill of Rights represented the spirit of revolutionary America, and they speak today with the same voice and continue to offer a measure by which the faithfulness of government is tested. The early colonists subscribed to the political system known as democracy because democracy provided a favorable climate for the growth and development of this "love of freedom." Democracy was not the source of this spirit of freedom. Similarly, a greenhouse provides the proper climate for the growth of flowers, but it is not the source of their life. No legal document gives birth to the individual's rights, duties, dignity, and equality—these come from the Creator. Man was meant to be free.

Within the framework of this spiritual belief comes the Supreme Court's view that the First Amendment has the purpose of reserving from all official control the sphere of intellect and spirit. Conscience and belief are the main ingredients of First Amendment rights. Without this Amendment we would degenerate into a police state. As Chief Justice Hughes stated in the *Macintosh* case: "But in the form of conscience, duty to a moral power higher than the state has always been maintained." (*United States v. Macintosh*, 283 U.S. 633, 51 S. Ct. 478 [1930].) Freedom of thought protected by the First Amendment against state action includes both the right to speak freely and the right to refrain from speaking. These rights are components of the broader concept of individual freedom of mind. There can be no freedom of the mind unless ideas can be uttered. That is the command of the First Amendment.

Although the Congress can make no law abridging the freedom of speech, press, or assembly, it has long been established "that these freedoms themselves are dependent upon the power of constitutional government to survive." Since the government has the right to protect itself against unlawful acts, the question arises when the government can suppress the freedom of speech which advocates conduct that may cause injury to the public welfare. The Supreme Court solved the potential conflicting interests between the freedom of the individual and the rights of the government by applying the "test" laid down in the *Schenck* case. Stated the Court: "The question in every case is whether the words are used in such circumstances and of such a nature as to create a clear and present danger that they will bring about the *substantive* evils that Congress has a right to prevent. [Emphasis added.]" (*Schenck v. United States*, 249 U.S. 52, 39 S. Ct. 249 [1919].)

The liberty of the press is indeed essential to the nature of a free society. William Blackstone, the illustrious English jurist, wrote, "Every freeman has an undoubted right to lay what sentiments he pleases before the public; to forbid this is to destroy the freedom of press." This right does not, however, imply freedom from penalty where injury is done by what is published. So Blackstone added that if anyone publishes "What is improper, mischievious or illegal, he must take the consequences of his temerity." Harmful conduct justifies restrictions upon speech and press when *substantial* interests of society are at stake.

The right of the public to be protected from the evils of harmful conduct has received consistent recognition by the Supreme Court, even though First Amendment rights of persons or groups are thereby in some manner infringed or their exercise restrained. Nothing in the Constitution prevents legitimate attempts to prevent potential injury to the public from harmfully active conduct. In a free society, however, it is imperative not to allow the public authority to employ this right to "regulate" conduct as a cloak to hide censorship of unpopular ideas. By accepting and abiding by certain restraints placed on individuals and on government alike, the delicate and fragile balance between the rights of the individual granted by the First Amendment and the rights of the government to protect the public welfare can be maintained.

Judge Jerre S. Williams, in his lecture "The First Amendment and the Mass Media," offers a scholarly survey of the state of the law dealing with First Amendment rights. In examining the question whether the press has special rights other than those enjoyed by all citizens, he concludes that the press has no such rights. Pointing out that newspapers and other publications are privately owned businesses with no formal responsibility to the public, and pointing out that the press in the United States enjoys a latitude experienced in no other country in the world, Judge Williams sees no reason to extend a special, ombudsman-like role to the press.

Judge Williams also takes up the question of the broadcast media and acknowledges that there are special limitations to the freedom of the electronic press due to the nature of the licensing procedure

necessarily imposed on scarce channels available for
radio and television broadcast. One of the most difficult problems today in the laws affecting the freedom
of the press is reconciling such governmental control
with the liberty of expression granted by the First
Amendment.

One of the surest safeguards of liberty is conscience.
Conscience is often the echo of religious faith. The
term "religion" has reference to one's views of his
relation to his Creator, and the question as to what
belief in superhuman power is correct is beyond the
jurisdiction of any court. This belief has to do with the
entirely personal nature of the religious experience
and performance of every human being. "In France,"
wrote Alexis de Tocqueville in *Democracy in America*
(1839), "I had almost always seen the spirit of religion
and the spirit of freedom marching in opposite directions. But in America I found they were intimately
united and they reigned over the same country." One
of the rights that are unalienable—which the government cannot take away and the citizen need not ever
surrender—is the freedom of religion.

Jefferson's bill for Establishing Religious Freedom
offered full religious liberty and freedom from coercion in matters of conscience. The bill, which went far
beyond the wishes of mere advocates of toleration,
proclaimed: "Well aware . . . that Almighty God hath
created the mind free, and manifested his supreme
will that free it shall remain by making it altogether
insusceptible of restraint . . . We the General Assembly of Virginia do enact that no man shall be compelled
to frequent or support any religious worship, place, or
ministry whatsoever, nor shall be enforced, res-

trained, molested, or burthened in his body or goods, nor shall otherwise suffer, on account of religious opinions or belief; but that all men shall be free to profess, and by argument to maintain, their opinions in matters of religion, and at the same shall in no wise diminish, enlarge, or affect their civil capacities . . ."

A distinction should be made between religious beliefs and religious practices. In a country which enjoys religious freedom, laws cannot interfere with religious beliefs and opinions, but these beliefs cannot serve as an excuse for religious practices that violate existing laws. Religious practices cannot become superior to the law of the land and thus permit every citizen to become a law unto himself. As our courts have stated:

> "Every individual has a natural and unalienable right to worship God, according to the dictates of his own conscience and reason; and it is also his 'natural and unalienable right' not to be 'hurt, molested, or restrained in his person, liberty, or estate, for worshipping God in the manner and season most agreeable to the dictates of his own conscience, or of his religious profession, sentiments, or persuasion, provided he does not disturb others." *(Hale v. Everett*, 53 N.H. 9, 16 Am. Rep. 82 [1868].)

Prof. Max L. Stackhouse, in his lecture "Religious Freedom and Human Rights: A 'Public Theological' Perspective," stresses that religious freedom is the most basic of all freedoms and that threats to religious freedom are presently threatening human rights. In Prof. Stackhouse's opinion, views of human rights that

emphasize civil liberties alone neglect the all important underpinning of those liberties in ultimate
values—in religious beliefs. Both the libertarianism of
the right and the liberationism of the left leave these
ultimate values out of their philosophies.

To guard against such reductionism, Prof. Stackhouse argues that those in positions of moral
authority—those with responsibilities in churches,
seminaries, and universities—must see to it that the
moral underpinnings of our society are laid bare. Such
persons have a duty to make it clear that the essential
moral questions of our time must be solved against a
background of spiritual understanding. Though there
are realms of faith which are properly private, theologians and other scholars must identify those moral
questions which bear on public policy and offer their
moral witness as to the truth.

While in a democratic society the widest scope is
allowed to the freedom of speech and to the freedom
of religion, the concommitant principle of academic
freedom is necessarily subject to conditions which
maintain the essential purpose of a university, which is
to seek the truth. Academic freedom is not a citizen's
birthright. It is a right enjoyed only by those who are
qualified to teach within their disciplines. This
requirement of meeting standards of qualification as
an indispensable condition of professional performance does not imply that academic freedom calls for
teaching generally accepted truths.

Socrates, to whom philosophy was a way of life and
who tried to arouse a love of truth and virtue, was in
399 B.C. brought to trial for corrupting the youth of
Athens. In 1616, the Copernican theory of the solar

system was denounced as dangerous to faith. Galileo was tried by the Inquisition and imprisoned for upholding the Copernican theory that the sun is the central body in the solar system and the earth a moving body revolving with the other planets around it.

A qualified person who seeks to fulfill the mission of a university by searching for truth has the right to reach conclusions that seem to him reasonably valid in the light of objective scholarship and intellectual integrity. This academic freedom carries with it duties correlative with rights. The 1940 Basic Statement on Academic Freedom of the American Association of University Professors states: "The teacher is entitled to freedom in the classroom in discussing his subject but should be careful not to introduce into his teaching controversial matter which has no relation to his subject." In 1956, the AAUP asserted, "The academic community has a duty to defend society and itself from subversion of the educational process by dishonest tactics, including political conspiracies to deceive students and lead them into acceptance of dogmas or false causes."

The concept of academic freedom originated at the University of Berlin in 1810. Today in the United States most colleges and universities adhere to the generally accepted principles associated with this freedom. The pursuit of truth is a noble intellectual end that can be obtained by those who accept duties and responsibilities as a correlative to the right of academic freedom. This freedom cannot be used as an immunity from sanctions against teachers' duties and responsibilities for excellence in teaching.

In his lecture "Academic Freedom and Responsibil-

ity: Moral Values on the Campus," Prof. Arvo Van
Alstyne examines the basis of academic freedom and
finds that it is not simply the freedom of speech which
is the right of every citizen. It is both more than and
less than that general liberty. It is broader than the
constitutional right to free speech, since it binds also
private institutions. But it is narrower, in that it applies to professional research only, and not to all areas
of thought and expression, unrelated to the academic
discipline of the teacher.

Prof. Van Alstyne also argues that those in academic
circles should realize that the purpose of academic
freedom is not merely to give job security. The focus
in thinking about and discussing academic freedom
must always remain the search for truth and the progress of knowledge. Only those scholars who exemplify the ideals embodied in such a search are
carrying out the responsibilities entailed by the claims
of academic freedom.

Economic freedom is another of many interrelated
freedoms guaranteed by the Constitution, and one—
though basic in the thoughts of our Founding
Fathers—that is often forgotten today in discussions of
the basic freedoms. It cannot be separated from the
other freedoms enjoyed under a constitutional government. The motives that lead men to cooperate or to
fight each other, to work to make the earth productive
or to be idle, to be provident or to live for the moment, are all motives which influence the ability to
produce and to distribute God's gifts in an adequate
way. The main social objectives—peace, freedom, and
progress—have a close relation to economic prosperity. The key to unlocking economic progress is free-

dom of the individual combined with concern for the welfare of his fellowman.

In my lecture on "Economic Freedom: The Rights and Responsibilities of the Entrepreneur in Our Mixed Economy," I have tried to point out that we live in one of the freest lands upon the earth and that in our generation we have witnessed convincing evidence in favor of the capitalist path to prosperity. It is essential for economic progress that business leadership provides a healthy combination of self-interest and an awareness of the public interest. If the businessman looks only toward acquisition of wealth for its own sake or toward attainment of power over others or of special privilege, then selfish desires take priority over his responsibility for the freedom and welfare of his fellowman. History provides evidence that what is morally wrong can never be economically right in the long run. Problems related to the economic order cannot be kept separate from sociopolitical problems.

Because of the efforts to link progress in the economy to success in the field of social reform, the Marxist prediction of the downfall of the capitalist system, which has been repeatedly stressed for over half a century by communist leaders in their bitter attacks on our system, has never materialized. The anticipated cataclysmic split of our society into two hostile camps or two antagonistic classes—the bourgeois and the labor—has never come. The communist hopes that the American economy would collapse in the common ruin of contending classes have proved to be ill-founded.

Economic prosperity has as one of its main goals the attainment of full employment. American labor repudiates the "security" and the "industrial peace" offered by communism. The price of that sort of "full employment" is coercive statism and slavery. The State imposes its will on the worker and regards him as an impersonal cog in a machine. The worker's freedom is lost and he becomes a serf of the State, instead of his government being a servant to him.

Labor relations have a direct impact on economic growth, inflation, international trade, energy, and stability of the economy. The survival of free unions and free management—which is the survival of competitive enterprise—depends on the establishment of working peace between management and union leadership. The challenge to find cooperative avenues can be met by common understanding of the rights and responsibilities of management and labor.

Prof. Ray Marshall, in his address "Labor in a Free Society," stresses the moral dimensions of all work, especially the dignity of labor and the need for economic justice. Government, in his view, has the responsibility to further these ends, as does the organized labor movement. He points out that the greatest power any group has is its moral impact. In order to be truly effective, labor has to convince others in our society that it desires to advance the common good rather than merely its own special interests.

Prof. Marshall is concerned about widening inequalities in wealth and income and the weakening influence of the organized labor movement. He believes that the answers to many practical problems our society faces are as much moral as practical and that a resort to principles of cooperation of all segments of our economy rather than confrontation would strengthen the bonds which tie us together. Flexibility, compromise, and unity are all principles that flow from the responsibility of both business and labor to seek a mutually just industrial peace.

Freedom must be defended at home by attending to the spirit of liberty that is enshrined within our Constitution and within our laws and traditions. Freedom must also be protected from those who would destroy it from the outside—and thus our national security is of its very essence.

Peace is attainable through strenuous negotiations which must fail if they are not undergirded by the power to defend our country. Power without negotiations and national self-assertion will not bring about the arrangements that an imaginative program of peace requires. A readiness to defend our country, combined with a policy that seeks equitable and meaningful agreements, seems to be the strategy which offers a hope of relieving the world from strife and dangers.

In his lecture "Morality and Pragmatism in Foreign Policy," Prof. Eugene V. Rostow stresses the close interrelation of strength and peace. In arguing that we must pursue peace aggressively, he concludes that the surest way to do so is not only to achieve military preparedness but to foster the network of military alliances that have preserved at least a modicum of peace over the last forty years through the balance of power. Peace is inherently fragile. It must be guarded vigilantly.

Stronger nations, like the United States, have in Prof. Rostow's view a special responsibility to maintain the peace. He fears that the other largest power, the

Soviet Union, is committed to aggression rather than to peaceful cooperation. Thus the United States has an even larger responsibility to all the nations of the world to do its utmost to preserve the balance of power and thus prevent war. No decisive aggregation of power inimical to the interests of world peace can be allowed to rise. Only by accepting this responsibility can the independence of the Free World be preserved.

In all the 1984 Lectures on Moral Values in a Free Society, the theme is repeatedly emphasized that we must face up to the issues involved in freedom and in the abuse of freedom. Freedom is among the most precious of all possessions, but it may turn into wild licentiousness when exercized without the full responsibility implied in citizenship. When it is combined with such responsibility, it enhances the spirit of the mutual dependence of human beings upon one another. It undergirds the structure of the brotherly relations of life with life, relations called the basic "law of life" by Reinhold Neihbur.

Only by our determination to preserve our rights to freedom and to carry out our responsibilities in a conscientious manner can our nation avoid the disintegration experienced by ancient societies. In 431 B.C., Pericles, commemorating the war dead of Athens, pointed out the road to greatness that had enabled the ancestors of the Athenians to hand down their country free from generation to generation in succession:

"Our constitution does not copy the laws of neighboring states; we are rather a pattern to others than imitators ourselves. Its administration favors the many instead of the few; this is why it is called a democracy. If we look to the laws, they afford equal justice to all in their private differences; if to social standing, advancement in public life falls to reputation for capacity, class considerations not being allowed to interfere with merit."

If we believe that our destiny is to serve through our conduct as an example to other nations and to our future generations, we have to choose this high road to greatness that the ancient Athenians followed and keep nourishing the spirit of liberty that is enshrined within our Constitution and within our laws and traditions.

THE FIRST AMENDMENT AND THE MASS MEDIA

by

Jerre S. Williams

Jerre S. Williams

Judge Williams is Circuit Judge of the United States Court of Appeals, Fifth Judicial Circuit. His appointment was confirmed on June 18, 1980, and he was sworn in on July 2, 1980.

Having received his A.B. from the University of Denver and his J.D. from Columbia Law School, Judge Williams served as Professor of Law at the University of Texas Law School from 1946 to 1980, and occupied the John B. Connally Chair of Civil Jurisprudence from 1970 to 1980. Among the subjects he taught were Administrative Law, Constitutional Law, Labor Relations, and the Legal Profession.

Judge Williams served as the first Chairman of the Administrative Conference of the United States from 1967 to 1970, as Chairman of the Southwestern Manpower Advisory Committee, and as a Consultant to the U.S. Bureau of the Budget. He was appointed by Presidents Johnson and Carter to Presidential Emergency Boards to settle nationwide strikes, and has held important offices in the National Academy of Arbitrators, the Association of American Law Schools, and the American Bar Association. He was the Research Fellows' Distinguished Scholar in Residence of The Southwestern Legal Foundation 1973 through 1977.

The author of numerous articles in legal publications, Judge Williams has also written Cases and Materials on Employee's Rights *(1952),* The Supreme Court Speaks *(1956), and* Constitutional Analysis *(Nutshell Series, 1979). He was the Principal Editor of* Labor Relations and the Law *(Third Edition, 1965).*

THE FIRST AMENDMENT AND THE MASS MEDIA

by

Jerre S. Williams

It is a rare privilege to participate in this sixth annual lecture series honoring Dr. Andrew Cecil. His has been a unique contribution to the understanding and enhancement of American freedom. The contributions have flowed from his creativity and administrative acumen in the many years he served as President of The Southwestern Legal Foundation. But they have also flowed from his intense personal scholarly production which is consistently of the highest order. I join with enthusiasm in honoring him this day.

Introduction

Our inquiry is directed to the content of the constitutional freedom of the press and also of the other mass media of communication which have been so richly developed in recent years. But in defining this freedom, we must define its limits as well. Implicit in the drawing of lines between what is lawful and what can be forbidden is an unavoidable emphasis upon what is forbidden. Lest such an emphasis should be taken to overshadow the constitutional protections which are here discussed, let me emphasize certain

propositions at the beginning which undergird all that
is to follow.

It is now customary to refer to these constitutional
protections as First Amendment protections, although
all students of constitutional history know that the
First Amendment when written applied only to the
federal government, and the United States Supreme
Court has used the Fourteenth Amendment Due
Process of Law Clause to make all important protections of the Bill of Rights applicable as restraints
also against the states. Even with that one sentence
history, it is somewhat of a shock to realize that it was
not until 135 years after the adoption of the Constitution, in 1925, that for the first time protections involved in First Amendment freedom of speech were
made applicable to the states through the Fourteenth
Amendment. The case was *Gitlow v. New York* (268
U.S. 652 [1925]). And it was not until 1940, in the case
of *Cantwell v. Connecticut* (310 U.S. 296 [1940]), that
the First Amendment freedom of religion was first
made applicable to state law. Our nation held its great
bicentennial celebration eight years ago. Yet, virtually
the entire history of legally enforced freedom of the
press in our country falls within the lifetime of some
persons who are hearing this lecture, and many who
will read its printed version.

So let me first state these basic propositions which
form the core of the freedom of the press and other
mass media of communication:

(1) Freedom of speech and press insures the
right freely to criticize the policies and activities of

the governments of the United States and of the states and their subdivisions. The right to criticize through ideas and opinion is virtually complete. Only when there is movement beyond criticism into the area of dangerous and immediate incitement to serious lawbreaking—that is, riot, physical danger to the populace, or ultimate revolution—do we place a limitation upon the right to criticize governmental policies.

(2) The right to criticize public officials and their activities is limited only by making illegal the publication of knowing or recklessly malicious falsehoods. The publication of opinions as to the quality, activities, and policies of public officials is unrestricted.

(3) A broader proposition establishes that freedom of the press does not in general require that the statements made by the media be true. Just as we properly fall far short of requiring candidates for political offices to say only the truth, we do not hold the media to a standard of absolute truth either. And this is important to press freedom. If absolute truth were required of the media at all times and in all of its statements, the social costs of checking and rechecking, as well as the dilemma of deciding what is presented as factual truth and what is not, would literally destroy the freedom of the media to act quickly and effectively in communicating news and views to the people.

(4) In general, the freedom of the media includes subject matter freedom—the right to present information as to what is happening around

us with only infrequently applicable restrictions based upon governmental information which must be kept secret and limitations based upon our concepts of defamation and obscentiy.

These propositions are broad generalizations. They are advanced here only to stress at the beginning the breadth of the freedom which we give the media. Our press freedom, it confidently can be stated, is not surpassed, nor probably even equalled, anywhere else in the world.

As I enter my subject matter to cover in a relatively few minutes what could easily take a large volume, I am of necessity restricted to certain highlights. Further, I shall undertake to say enough things that might be reasonably provocative to some of you to avoid presenting only a compendium.

The starting point for evaluation of freedom of the press is found in two intense common-law restrictions upon press freedom. The first of these was the well-established principle of press licensing. Development in reaction to the licensing principle in turn brought about the freedom from prior restraint upon publication. The second common-law restriction upon press freedom was the blanket criminal offense created to punish those who criticized the actions of the State and its officers, the crime of "seditious libel." Developmental reaction to seditious libel led to the modern definitions of free speech and free press.

In the context of free speech and free press, the application of the principle prohibiting prior restraints precedes the decision as to whether a particular utterance, be it by a person, by the press in the classic sense of the printed word, or by the electronic media, is something which can be prohibited by the government in the face of the constitutional protection of the First Amendment. So we turn our attention first to the important principle limiting prior restraint, or censorship, upon speech and the press.

Prior Restraint

Freedom of the press had to shake the shackles of the established British concept that the press was licensed by the State and authorized to act only in accordance with that State restricted license. The doctrine prohibiting prior restraint was created to get around this harsh principle. By eliminating absolute censorship by the State, the distributed material could be published, although this meant that the publisher ran the risk that a jury would later find the material had been published in violation of law. But at least it could not be suppressed in advance by the State.

The protection was far from sweeping because, as Blackstone saw it, he contemplated no change in the ultimate responsibility for what was published. He only recognized the freedom from a prior restraint upon publication. Blackstone said:

"The liberty of the press is indeed essential to the nature of a free state; but this consists in laying no *previous* restraints upon publications, and not in freedom from censure for criminal matter when published. Every free man has an undoubted right to lay what sentiments he pleases before the public; to forbid this, is to destroy the freedom of the press; but if he publishes what is improper, mischievous, or illegal, he must take the consequence of his own temerity." (4 Bl. Com. 151, 152.)

Chief Justice Hughes in the leading early Supreme Court case on prior restraint, *Near v. Minnesota* (283 U.S. 697 [1931]), pushed beyond the Blackstonian analysis and emphasized the importance of constitutional protection from subsequent punishment for those statements not previously restrained. Thus the fundamental constitutional test of freedom of speech and of press is applied after the publication to determine if it is constitutionally privileged. The prior restraint issue is a preliminary issue which does not resolve the ultimate determination of the scope of the freedom. This does not mean, however, that no utterances at all can be subjected to prior restraint.

The great modern leading case on the application of the doctrine of prior restraint is, of course, the Pentagon Papers case, *New York Times v. United States* (403 U.S. 713 [1971]). You will recall that Daniel Ellsberg purloined a large number of documents classified as secret and confidential from the Pentagon files while he was working there. This was part of his personal drive to undermine the American efforts in Viet Nam. These papers came into the hands of *The New York Times* and the *Washington Post*. Suit was brought by the government to restrain the publication of some of those papers. The Supreme Court denied the government's demand that their publication be enjoined.

The case has never received adequate treatment in the press for reasons which will become clear in a moment. What actually is involved in that case is exceedingly important to an evaluation of the concept of prior restraint. The case was argued on behalf of the United States Government by Solicitor General Erwin Griswold. To most of us, Griswold is still "Dean Griswold" because of his many distinguished years as Dean of the Harvard Law School. Dean Griswold gave a fascinating account of the case of *New York Times v. United States* to the Convention of the Association of American Law Schools assembled in New York in 1972. This is an account which I have not seen anywhere else, yet it is essential to a full understanding of what happened in the case. Dr. Griswold's address can be found tucked away in *Association of American Law Schools, 1972, Proceedings,* Part II, Annual Meeting, p. 73.

Dean Griswold reported that out of the forty-seven volumes which consisted of the "Pentagon Papers," the government picked out eleven documents which it felt were of such serious prejudice to the United States that their publication could properly be enjoined. It is a matter of significant interest, and, I believe, not reported in the press, that *The New York Times* and the *Washington Post* conceded that there were other documents which were so sensitive they were subject to prior restraint and which were not placed in issue in the case.

I might add as a brief aside that Dean Griswold's story of the case contains some absurd situations growing out of the government's rather footless attempt to maintain security with respect to the documents. For example, the government tried to keep Dean Griswold's secretary from working on the case because she did not have a security clearance. He handled this in typical Griswold fashion by simply telling the security officer to go back and tell his superiors that Dean Griswold would not pay any attention to him. Then Dean Griswold received a call after one of the trial days from the attorney for the newspapers saying he would like to see a copy of the secret brief. Each party had filed a secret brief as well as an open brief. Dean Griswold replied that he had handed him a secret brief in court the day before. But the attorney for the newspaper said that the security man came around and took it away from him because it was a secret document and he did not have security clearance and the need to know. So the lawyer had not been able to see it.

Back to the critical part of the case. The government lost with respect to all eleven documents by the 6-to-3 decision of the Supreme Court. But as Dean Griswold revealed, the incredible and not known fact is that neither newspaper printed a single one of those eleven documents after the case was won! This leaves a fascinating question. Did *The New York Times* and the *Washington Post* feel such a sense of concern for the well-being of our country that they decided on their own that it was better not to print those documents? Or did they act on the basis of legal advice that the failure of the government to get an injunction against their publication did not legalize their publication in any way, and the newspapers would be just as criminally liable subsequently if they published government documents which deserved the secret classification?

No matter which was the reason, we are given two important lessons from this chain of events. The first, of course, is the one that I just mentioned, the failure to issue a prior restraint against the publication of these documents did not legalize their publication. These were stolen documents, and as Chief Justice Burger said in his dissent, why should the press be any freer from cooperating with the government to return stolen government property which comes in its hands than anyone else? This question is relevant to the later discussion of whether the press has protections over and above those of each citizen when it claims freedom of press and the citizen claims freedom of speech.

The other lesson is that the importance of a free and militant press does not and should not overshadow the fact that the ultimate decisions as to confidentiality and national security must rest in the government. Having been in government positions where I have seen and handled confidential information, I have considerable doubt about the wisdom of the government retaining much of what it calls secrets as actually secret. Yet, when the choice must be made between our government making that decision on behalf of the people and a private, for profit, enterprise making that decision, on balance I firmly believe the government must prevail. I do not want to submit ultimate issues of national security and confidentiality to the press for its decision. Our government processes may be far from perfect, but they are ours. They inescapably must more readily reflect the wishes and needs of the people than do the decisions of the privately operated media over which the people generally have virtually no control, and properly so.

We can live safely with the decision of the Supreme Court in *New York Times v. United States*. With the exception of Justices Black and Douglas—who took the absolutist position that no prior restraint is ever justified, a position which is clearly not the law, as the *Washington Post* and *The New York Times* conceded—the issue involves a careful balancing of the damage which can be done by publication as against the important role that criticizing the government plays in any free society. The determination must be on a case-by-case basis.

It is rather remarkable to note that in the *United States v. Marchetti* (466 F.2d 1309 [4th Cir. 1972]), the Supreme Court denied *certiorari* (409 U.S. 1063 (1972]), just eighteen months after the decision in the *Times* case. The Fourth Circuit in that case held that Marchetti, a former CIA employee, could be enjoined from publishing classified information in a book he was writing about the agency, contrary to his promises contained in his employment contract. Note that the contract was not the basis of the Fourth Circuit's decision, however, because the Court refused to enjoin the publication of nonclassified information in the book although this was also in breach of contract.

We must remind ourselves also that the doctrine of prior restraint is not limited in its application to situations in whch the press is contemplating publishing material which belongs to the government. We have the issue of prior restraint in general criticism of the government as in the early *Near v. Minnesota* case. We have the issue whenever there is an exercise of speech which may not be subject to constitutional protection. In obscenity we have not allowed the general application of a prior restraint, but we do allow the licensing and censorship of motion pictures under carefully controlled circumstances which require that the censorship order must be taken before a magistrate in time to allow the magistrate to overturn the order before the performance is to take place. *(Freedman v. Maryland*, 380 U.S. 51 (1965].) By the same token it can properly be assumed that material to be presented on radio and television is not subject to prior restraint unless some seriously overriding danger to the government is involved, such as that which justifies wartime censorship of troop movements and military plans.

The reason the doctrine prohibiting prior restraints is so important to the freedom of speech and press is because it enables the charged material to get before the public. Public evaluation can then act effectively upon unreasonable as well as unconstitutional governmental restraints, as is perhaps most commonly manifested in the overclassification of governmental documents.

Scope of Substantive Freedom of Speech

If there is no issue of prior restraint, we then move to the core constitutional issue of the media freedoms to express themselves through news, editorial opinion, interviews, and, in some cases we must admit, pure gossip.

As mentioned briefly earlier, the origin of press freedom grows out of the struggle against the licensing of the press and the prohibition against "seditious libel" which pragmatically was nothing but a dramatic phrase to refer to criticism of the government which the government wished to suppress. As you know, we at one time had the spectacle of the United States Government trying to bring the concept of seditious libel into American criminal jurisprudence in spite of the First Amendment. In 1798, the Sedition Act was enacted. That Act made it a felony "if any person shall write, print, utter, or publish . . . any false, scandalous and malicious writing or writings against the government of the United States or either house of the Congress . . ., of the President . . ., with intent to defame . . . or bring them, or either of them to contempt or disrepute; or to excite against them or either or any of them the hatred of the good people of the United States."

It was not until *New York Times v. Sullivan* (376 U.S. 276 [1964]), the leading case on libel as against First Amendment rights, that the Supreme Court in a majority opinion stated that the Sedition Act had been unconstitutional. Justice Holmes, however, in an eloquent and famous dissent in *Abrams v. United States* (250 U.S. 616, 630 [1919]), had said that he "wholly disagreed with the argument of the government that the First Amendment left the common law as to seditious libel in force." He went on to say that the United States had shown through many years its repentance for the Sedition Act of 1798 by repaying the fines which had been imposed under that law. Finally, he said "only the emergency that makes it immediately dangerous to leave the correction of evil counsels to time warrants making any exception to the sweeping command" of the First Amendment. This, of course, was a later formulation in words of his clear and present danger test which he created in his majority opinion in *Schenck v. United States* (249 U.S. 47 [1919]) earlier in the same year.

In a few words, then, the common-law concept of seditous libel is replaced by the First Amendment protection of freedom of speech and press unless the utterances constitute a clear and present danger of the evils which the government has the right to prevent. (*Id.* at 52.)

This is still the constitutional test in cases which involve the issue of subversive speech or, as in the case of the Pentagon Papers, speech which can undermine the basic national security of the United States. The test was applied in the Smith Act (18 U.S.C. § 2385) prosecutions of the leaders of the Communist Party in *Dennis v. United States.* (341 U.S. 494, 508 [1951].)

Hyperanalysts seem to abound particularly in evaluating constitutional decisions. Some of them have argued that the 1969 case of *Brandenberg v. Ohio* weakened the clear and present danger test. This was a case which involved vituperative advocacy by members of the Ku Klux Klan which also included vague threats of illegal activity. The case set aside the convictions. It must not be taken, however, as a weakening of the clear and present danger test because neither the indictment nor the trial judge's instructions to the jury in any way made a distinction between mere advocacy as distinguished from "incitement to imminent lawless action." Thus, clear and present danger was never put in issue. (*Brandenberg v. Ohio*, 395 U.S. 444 [1969].)

Is Free Press Broader Than Free Speech?

We have now laid the foundation for a more detailed evaluation of freedom of the press by setting out its two basic lines of development, the prior restraint and the elimination of the doctrine of seditious libel. Most of our constitutional analysis of free speech comes from attempts by the various states to regulate speech and press. After the Sedition Act of 1798, the Congress got itself out of the business of trying to regulate free speech until the World War I cases which developed the clear and present danger test. In the meantime, the many-faceted controls of free speech grew out of state activities. Governmental attempts to control free speech in the modern era are largely attempts by the states to control. I remind you as I said at the beginning that the First Amendment was not made applicable to the states except in the lifetime of some of you who are here—135 years after the adoption of the Constitution.

There is a third and final important line in the development of the meaning of freedom of press under the First Amendment. There is intense controversy today over the specific reference to freedom of press in the Amendment. The First Amendment reads, "Congress shall make no law . . . abridging the freedom of speech, or of the press . . ." The limitation as to Congress has disappeared under the Fourteenth Amendment, as just mentioned. The issue is: Does the reference to freedom of the press differentiate it from freedom of speech and give the press greater liberties under the First and Fourteenth Amendment than those which apply to citizens generally? The view that freedom of the press is a broader protection of liberty than freedom of speech is espoused by several recent writers and has been referred to at least indirectly by one recent member of the Supreme Court.

It is my view that those who find an additional grant of freedom to the press over and beyond the freedom given to the citizens generally under freedom of speech either do not know history at all or are historical revisionists. That perhaps may be unduly harsh, because there could be a third alternative which I shall mention briefly later, that the content of freedom of the press may change under a living, growing, and changing Constitution.

History tells us without any question that the insertion of freedom of the press in the First Amendment was to bring press freedom up to the level of citizen freedom of speech—not to go beyond. The press had been subject to licensing—to censorship. The purpose of making reference to the press was to ensure that the organized press and the pamphleteers also had freedom of speech as against intrusion from the federal government. The historical studies of that period make this clear, e.g., Levy, *Legacy of Suppression:*

Freedom of Speech and Press in Early American History, Ch. 5.

This is not just my view, it is the clearly established law of the land as proclaimed by the Supreme Court. Even if I personally felt otherwise, as a Judge of the United States Court of Appeals I would be bound to follow this principle of law. The major pronouncement on this issue is in the Supreme Court case of *Branzburg v. Hayes* (408 U.S. 665 [1972]), which denied newspaper reporters the right to conceal their sources of confidential information when subpoenaed to appear before a Grand Jury investigating criminal activity. In that case the Court said:

> "It has generally been held that the First Amendment does not guarantee the press a constitutional right of special access to information not available to the public generally. . . . Newsmen have no constitutional right of access to the scenes of crime or disaster when the general public is excluded . . ." (*Id.* at 684.)

This principle is echoed in a dissenting opinion by Justice Powell in which—and this is significant—Justices Brennan and Marshall joined. In *Saxbe v. Washington Post Co.* (417 U.S. 843 (1974]), the Supreme Court held that the media had no additional access to interviews with criminals serving prison terms than did the public generally. Justice Powell urged a pragmatic conclusion that it was impossible to allow the public access but that the news media could be allowed access under carefully controlled conditions as representatives of the public. But in drawing this conclusion he said:

> "I agree, of course, that neither any news organization nor reporters as individuals have constitutional rights superior to those enjoyed by ordinary citizens. The guarantees of the First Amendment broadly secure the rights of every citizen; they do not create special privileges for particular groups or individuals. For me, at least, it is clear that persons who become journalists acquire thereby no special immunity from government regulation." *(Id.* at 857.)

Further the distinguished Pulitzer Prize winner journalist Anthony Lewis characterizes the case of *Richmond Newspapers v. Virginia* (448 U.S. 555 [1980]) as settling once and for all the claim of the press that it is entitled to greater privilege than citizens generally. (1980 The Supreme Court Review 19.) This is the important case which upheld the right of public and media to attend criminal trials. The defense had moved that the trial be closed to the public, and the prosecutor did not disagree. The Supreme Court, however, held in an 8-to-1 decision that the public, including the media, had the right of access to the trial. The critical point in the case for our purposes is that the media was treated as not being entitled to any greater access than the public, although the case did not deny the right of such practical arrangements as having a special press section in the courtroom.

In one case, Justice Stewart sent up a trial balloon seemingly recognizing possible validity to the theory that because of the separate listing of free press in the First Amendment the press was entitled to certain privileges that the citizen did not have. The case, *Zurcher v. The Stanford Daily* (436 U.S. 547 [1978]), is the one in which the university student newspaper brought a civil rights action seeking declaratory and injunctive relief against police officers and others conducting a search of the newspaper premises for pictures revealing the identity of demonstrators who assaulted police officers during a student confrontation at Stanford. The majority of the Court upheld the search warrant in an opinion by Justice White. Justice Stewart dissented in an opinion in which he said that newspapers were entitled to be searched only by subpoena rather than a search warrant because a search warrant allowed the police to rummage around in the files of the newspaper. He went on to say that protection of the confidential sources "is necessary to ensure that the press can fulfill its constitutionally designated function of informing the public . . ." (*Id.* at 571.)

Justice Powell wrote a concurring opinion. But he said that the sole purpose of writing separately was to emphasize the "fundamental error" of Justice Stewart's dissenting opinion. He went on to say: "If the Framers had believed that the press was entitled to a special procedure, not available to others, when government authorities required evidence in its possession, one would have expected the terms of the Fourth Amendment to reflect that belief." (*Id.* at 569.) In contrast, Justice Stewart, just a month later in *Houghins v. KQED, Inc.* (438 U.S. 1 [1978]), became more traditional in a concurring opinion in a case involving access to prison facilities by the media, He there expressed agreement with the controlling constitutional principle by saying:

> "The First and Fourteenth Amendments do not guarantee the public a right of access to information generated or controlled by government, nor do they guarantee the press any basic right of access superior to that of the public generally. The Constitution does no more than assure the public and the press equal access once government has opened its doors." *(Id.* at 16.)

It therefore seems reasonably clear that the established principle that press freedom does not extend beyond the citizen's freedom of speech is the proper constitutional interpretation absent any recognition of a possible future modification of the First Amendment through the concept of a living, growing, expanding Constitution. We properly must recognize that the concept of a changing and expanding Constitution is not alien to American constitutional principles. Chief Justice Hughes' statement said it most clearly in *Homebuilding & Loan Ass'n v. Blaisdell* (290 U.S. 398 [1934]).

> "If by the statement that what the Constitution meant at the time of its adoption it means today, it is intended to say that the great clauses of the Constitution must be confined to the interpretation which the framers, with the conditions and outlook of their time would have placed upon

them, the statement carries its own refutation. It was to guard against such a narrow concept that Chief Justice Marshall uttered the memorable warning—'we must never forget that it is a Constitution we are expounding' (*McCulloch v. Maryland,* 4 Wheat. 316, 407)—'a Constitution intended to endure for ages to come, and consequently, to be adapted to the various crises of human affairs.' " (*Id.* at 415.)

So there is a genuine issue as to whether we should now recognize that the press has greater rights than citizens generally with respect to freedom of expression. To me, however, the resolution of that issue is made clear merely by its statement. To build greater rights into a private business, usually a corporation organized for profit and fully aware of the need for profit, than those rights of American citizens generally to obtain information and to speak does not comport with freedom. There is no denying that the press is not democratic. It wholly controls the amount of citizen input which it wishes to recognize. As Dean Barrett of the University of California Law School has said:

> "The First Amendment used as a shield against government control, it seems to me, is its central meaning, and the press ought to hang very hard on the First Amendment as a shield. But when, dressed in the gleaming armour of Sir Galahad, the press not only has the shield up there with the First Amendment emblazoned on it, but also the sword, and wants to use the First Amendment as a device for compelling access to government in-

formation, for providing all kinds of special positions for the press—I think that poses the real danger." *(The Press: Free and Responsible?* Purvis, Ed., Symposium, Lyndon Baines Johnson Library and the Univ. of Texas 43 [1982].)

To the further claim that the press fulfills an ombudsman-like function—troubleshooting for citizens against the government—it is well to point out that the ombudsman is a government official. In the statement quoted above from Dean Barrett, the spectre of government control of the newspapers is obvious. If the newspapers are to be given a constitutionally designated function of informing the public, as is urged by those who advocate additional content to freedom of the press over freedom of speech, this can only mean a quasi-governmental function by the press. In turn this jeopardizes press independence and pushes toward government control of aspects of the press.

The dangers seem far to exceed the advantages when we begin to talk in terms of a special heightened content to press freedom. Freedom of the press must include freedom to be irresponsible in the sense that what is irresponsible is in the eyes of the beholder. Criticisms of government activities and individuals which seem irresponsible to some of us seem competent, effective, and important to others.

By mentioning freedom to be irresponsible, I do not urge irresponsibility on the press. I simply point out that freedom of speech and press means that the media need not be answerable for what they say and do except in the narrow limits of obscenity, libel, and

genuine danger of violence and threat to security. By
recognizing this media freedom we are assuring that
the government must stay out of the kind of controversy that arose in the *Washington Post* feature
"Jimmy's World" which was later exposed to be a
fictional account of drug addition in a child and which
caused the newspaper to return the Pulitzer prize
which had been awarded for the story. We do not have
to get into the controversy over "the new journalism"
which places more emphasis upon literary style, perhaps at the expense of accuracy. We do not need to get
into the controversy over "ambush" journalism where
we would be required to evaluate the extent to which
the media should sandbag public figures by arranging
interviews and then springing questions and information on them not anticipated. Nor do we need to
evaluate the full ramifications of modern "in-
vestigative" journalism.

I am talking today of constitutional rights. I am not
talking today of the responsibilities of the press as they
extend beyond those constitutional rights. That is a
wholly different topic, and it was the major thrust of
the Symposium which brought about Dean Barrett's
remarks which I quoted earlier. The leading pro-
tagonist for press responsibility in that Symposium
was the syndicated columnist Joseph Kraft. He constantly urged self-examination and actions of self-
responsibility. The press should continually reevalu-
ate their responsibilities and performance, and certainly the more responsible elements do. I simply
urge that we must continue to remind ourselves that
these are the responsibilities of private, money-

making organizations in our society, although they are organizations which undoubtedly fulfill an important public need. By talking some realism about the legal status of the press, I do not in any way intend to hint that the press does not play its important role in our society.

Defamation

As we speak of limitations upon press freedom, we must turn to a brief look at defamation because of its importance in any role that the press and the media play in our society. In the great case of *New York Times v. Sullivan* (376 U.S. 254 [1964]), the Supreme Court gave the American media a freedom to criticize which extends substantially beyond that to be found anywhere else in the world. It held that public officials and public figures cannot recover damages against media for any criticisms by way of opinion. As Justice Powell said in *Gertz v. Robert Welch, Inc.* (481 U.S. 323, 339 [1974]), "Under the First Amendment there is no such thing as a false idea. However pernicious an opinion may seem, we depend for its correction not on the conscience of judges and juries but on the competition of other ideas. But there is no constitutional value in false statements of fact." When actual falsehoods are involved, the *Sullivan* opinion said:

"The constitutional guarantees require, we think, a federal rule that prohibits a public official from recovering damages for a defamatory falsehood related to his official conduct unless he proves that

the statement was made with 'actual malice'—that
is, with knowledge that it was false or with reckless
disregard of whether it was false or not." (376 U.S.
at 279.)

Three Justices, Black, Douglas, and Goldberg,
would have gone further and asserted "an absolute
immunity for criticism of the way public officials do
their public duty." (*Id.* at 295, 298.) It is my personal
view, however, that the attempt to create absolutes
anywhere in the law is dangerous. Here, I disagree
with those who would create an absolute immunity
from responsibility for the defamation of public officials. I can foresee a wholly fabricated story against
an incumbent public official the day before the elec-
tion charging in specific and very precise terms the
theft of public funds, the use of the public office for
private gain in many ways, the committing of crimes
against the public good—with no time whatsoever to
rebut. And all, as I say, a total fabrication. The absolutist would say there would be no damages for this
action, and the media are arguing this position again in
General Westmoreland's case against CBS. I cannot
agree with this. The rule of *New York Times v. Sullivan* is broad and is, as I say, broader protection of the
media than is to be found anywhere else in the entire
world. We need not push beyond it.
    We have gone on to apply the same standard in the
"false light" cases where people who are not usually
prominent in the public eye have been thrust into
prominence by a newsworthy event. We give the protection to the newspaper so that it need not be
meticulous to the point of fear of making a mistake in

saying something not demonstrably true but not defamatory in such on-the-spot news stories. *(Times, Inc. v. Hill,* 385 U.S. 374 [1967].)

Further, in *New York Times v. Sullivan,* the Court created two additional significant protections for the press. It eschewed the application of the usual civil lawsuit standard for proof by a preponderance of the evidence and required that the malice requisite to recovery had to be proved with "convincing clarity." Then, second, the Court held that an appellate court must review independently a finding of malice against the press; it cannot, as it usually does, assume that the lower court decision is correct absent an affirmative showing of error. The review by the Court itself of the adequacy of evidence to prove malice by convincing clarity has just been reaffirmed by the Supreme Court in *Bose Corp v. Consumers Union of the U.S., Inc.* (104 S. Ct. 1949 [1984].)

As to private citizens as opposed to public figures, the *Gertz v. Robert Welch, Inc.* case, *supra,* held that the traditional common-law standard of defamation still continued, that the publication of false defamatory statements did entitle the person defamed to recover damages. It placed an additional strict limitation upon the common-law principle of recovery for defamation, however, by prohibiting the recovery of punitive damages. Only recovery of actual damage can be awarded in the absence of malice.

The media are disquieted by the 1979 Supreme Court case of *Herbert v. Landou* (441 U.S. 153). This is a case involving Viet Nam and criticism of Herbert, an army officer, on the CBS program "60 Minutes." Landou produced and edited the critical segment of the program. When his deposition was taken he was questioned about his activities, intent, and subjective knowledge as he was preparing the program. The lower court denied this right to inquire. This, of course, placed great inhibition upon the right of the plaintiff to prove knowing or reckless falsehood by the publication. The Supreme Court reversed, stressing the importance of placing all the evidence before the tribunal. It refused to create an evidentiary privilege as to these matters in the litigation context. The Court relied in part upon its holding in *United States v. Richard Nixon* (418 U.S. 683 [1974]), pointing out that even the President of the United States could not maintain confidentiality of activities within his own private office in the face of demonstrated specific need for evidence. In a word, the Court has a right to inquire into the editorial processes of the media to evaluate reckless disregard for the truth.

Disquietude or not, without this right to inquire there would be an almost insurmountable barrier facing a public official or public figure attacking the publication of a defamatory falsehood. There are serious dangers in inquiring into the editorial process in such cases, as Justice Brennan pointed out effectively in his dissent. But the balance falls on the side of full exploration of the evidence and denial of special privilege until grave intrusions on media freedom have become revealed. In Britain, every newspaper has a barrister on the payroll to evaluate in every edition every story which might possibly constitute defamation. Our newspapers are quite sensitive and vocal about their prerogative of being able to publish without undue obstacles in their discussion of public affairs. On balance, I reaffirm again we lean more strongly in their favor than anywhere else in the world.

The Electronic Media

Thus far, the discussion has centered upon the fundamental constitutional protections to the free press. The development of the electronic media leads us into a host of new questions centering about their licensing requirements. They are best demonstrated by the case of *Columbia Broadcasting System v. Democratic National Committee* (412 U.S. 94 [1973]). This is the case which held that the Columbia Broadcasting System had the right to refuse to sell advertising time for political broadcasts. The CBS policy was not discriminatory; it simply refused to sell time to all such applicants for purchased air time on the network.

The case starkly poses the problems associated with the electronic media when a reading of the opinions reveals that both the majority and the dissenters assert that theirs is the view which comports with constitutional freedom of speech! For the majority, it is the freedom of the Columbia Broadcasting System to speak or not as it wishes. For the dissenters, it is the freedom of those running for political office to make their public statements and be heard. The holding of the majority is the traditional free speech approach. The dissenters because of the licensed status of the electronic media depart from traditional free speech requirements. We do not and cannot force the printed press to publish something it does not want to publish. It is frightening to even think that a state law at-

tempted to force newspapers to give a right of reply to
a candidate to answer criticism. Such a law is foreign
to all free press concepts and was unanimously declared unconstitutional in *Miami Herald Pub. Co. v.
Tornillo* (418 U.S. 241 [1974]). Yet in *Red Lion
Broadcasting Co. v. FCC* (395 U.S. 367 [1969]), the
Supreme Court upheld the FCC's "fairness" doctrine,
forcing the radio station to give free time to someone
to answer personal attacks. The dissenters in CBS
dissented because the electronic media are licensed
by the government and licensing inescapably intrudes
the government into a supervisory role of the content
of the electronic media.

The majority of the Court in the *CBS v. Democratic
National Committee* case did not deny the government's role of licensing and control, it simply
walked the tightrope of allowing as much constitutional freedom as possible under such a system.
And therein lies the dilemma of the electronic media.
The channels of radio and television are limited in
number. They are owned by the people. The government must control who uses them. The government
licenses through the Communications Act under a
standard of "public interest, convenience, and necessity," an unthinkable concept in the case of the printed
press. The spectre that is raised, of course, is the
extent to which the government can and should control the content of the electronic media broadcasts
under its licensing requirements.

Again, in the last few years, there has been a revisionists' drive to insist that the electronic media
should be given exactly the same First Amendment
freedoms as the printed media. The argument is that

as a practical matter there is more competition in the radio and television business today than there is in the newspaper and printed media business. This pragmatic analysis, however, is wrecked on the rock of the licensing necessity itself. Radio and television stations are valuable assets. They exist only because the government licenses them to exist. Although some would quarrel, there probably is nothing in the Constitution that would forbid the United States Government from adopting a British system of wholly government owned and operated radio and television. How are our licensees to be chosen? The most justifiable standard would seem to be one of the public interest. Public interest can only be determined by programming plans which are submitted by the various applicants for licenses. Then there is the problem of monitoring those programming plans once the license is granted, since licenses come up for renewal frequently.

All this is thin ice, indeed, for genuine freedom of the electronic news media. Some have proposed that licenses be granted by lot. It has even been proposed that they be sold to the highest bidders. Even this does not solve our problem because either such a license would then have to be in perpetuity, or renewal would still raise the questions of continuity in the licensee with all of the issues concerning goodwill buildup and the expensive equipment involved. The FCC has even sanctioned a device, which has grown up in recent years, of rival applicants for a license reaching a settlement in which all but one of the applicants will withdraw, the one applicant remaining paying off the rival applicants ostensibly for their expenses in preparing their applications.

Thus, the precarious nature of the free press balance in the electronic media must continue. Again, this is not just a personal view. It is the law as declared by the Supreme Court.

The Supreme Court just this year had reconsidered the fundamental issues involved in spectrum scarcity and governmental licensing of the electronic media. The case is *FCC v. League of Women Voters of California* (104 S. Ct. 3106 [1984]). That case held unconstitutional a provision of the Public Broadcasting Act of 1967 (47 U.S.C. § 390 *et seq.*), which prohibited "editorializing" by any noncommercial educational broadcasting station receiving grants from the Corporation for Public Broadcasting. The statute, poorly conceived, was found defective for a number of detailed reasons, including its discriminatory impact on noncommercial stations and its peculiar application in that it did not prohibit stations from presenting partisan views on controversial matters, it simply forbade them from labeling them as their own. To the claim that Congress wanted to avoid subsidizing public broadcasting station editorials, the Court emphasized that the ban applied to a station which received only one percent of its income from the Corporation for Public Broadcasting.

For our purposes, the critical aspect of this case is that Justice Brennan in his opinion for the Court firmly recognized the continuing application of the concept of spectrum scarcity. He called the availability of the radio and televisions channels of communication "a scarce and valuable natural resource." (*Id.* at 3116.) He stressed the fact that the statute requires that the radio and television broadacast frequencies must be used in the public interest, convenience, and necessity. He even discussed the recent criticism of the assertion of spectrum scarcity, but went on to say that the Court was not prepared to reconsider its long-standing approach. Further, he confirmed the right in Congress in exercising its power to seek to assure a balanced presentation of information. Justices Rehnquist, Burger, White, and Stevens dissented. To them there was a genuine concern that government funds were being used to propagandize, and Congress had a right to control it.

The critical conclusion we draw, however, is the recognition in broadcasting of the governmental licensing power and measured control over content. Then we recognize the Court's desire to find constitutional underpinning for as much freedom for the broadcasting media under the First Amendment as is compatible with such a system of control.

The Federal Communications Commission is engaged in an attempt to deregulate the broadcast industry as much as possible. In doing so it has lowered its standards for the renewal of television licenses. The lowered standards have raised genuine concern among minority and other consumer groups. In *Black Citizens for a Fair Media v. FCC* (719 F.2d 407 [D.C. Cir. 1983]), the Court of Appeals for the District of Columbia upheld the validity of the FCC's less stringent renewal standards against the assertions of the minority group that those standards led to inadequate supervision of the requirement that the stations meet the public interest, convenience, and necessity. Intervening in the case was the Office of Communications of the United Church of Christ which had pioneered

citizens' rights to participate in TV license renewal in
two landmark opinions by then Judge Burger, now
Chief Justice Burger. (*Office of Communications of
the United Church of Christ v. FCC*, 359 F.2d 994
[D.C. Cir. 1966], and *Office of Communications of
United Church of Christ v. FCC*, 425 F.2d 543 [D.C.
Cir. 1969].)

The Court's decision in the *Black Citizens* case was
2-to-1 upholding the validity of the looser standards
required by the FCC for license renewal. Judge Bork
wrote the opinion for the Court, and Judge Skelley
Wright dissented. The Supreme Court denied *certiorari* in June 1984. (104 S. Ct. 3545.) But, a yellow
caution light is flashing. There are citizen groups who
feel strongly that their interests will not be represented by the electronic media if the government
ceases to demand programming which meets these
statutory standards. The issue remains.

Government Owned or Subsidized Media

The *League of Women Voters* case leads us into a
kind of speech issue demanding an increasingly important evaluation under the First Amendment. What if
the radio or TV station is owned and operated by the
public, by a governmental entity? This means that its
programming is the government speaking. Freedom
in that station could mean freedom to propagandize
officially. Yet we must recognize that the government
unavoidably plays an increasing role in expressing its
views through newspapers, pamphlets, and public an-
nouncements; the actual public ownership of broadcast media; and, of course, so broadly in public educa-

tion. This frontier area of First Amendment issues is effectively discussed in a recent seminal book by the Dean of the University of Texas Law School, Mark Yudof, *When Government Speaks.*

These special problems were posed very nicely in two cases in the United States Court of Appeals for the Fifth Circuit before it split into the Fifth and Eleventh Circuits. The cases are *Muir v. Alabama Educational Television Commission* and *Barnstone v. The University of Houston KUTH-TV* (688 F.2d 1033 [5th Cir. 1982]). In these two cases, the licensees, publicly owned broadcasting stations, decided not to broadcast an earlier scheduled controversial program entitled "Death of a Princess," which had been made the subject of an official protest by the Saudi Arabian government to the United States government. In both instances, the television stations had originally planned to broadcast the program and then decided not to do so. The decisions not to do so, of course, were made by governmental officials who played a role in the programming of the television stations.

Twenty-three judges sat en banc in the case. The majority of the Court held that the stations had the right to decide not to broadcast the particular program as against the claims of those potential viewers who had brought suit to force the stations to broadcast it. The opinion of the Court concluded that government stations could not claim First Amendment speech and press freedoms, but they still could claim the rights given them in the Broadcasting Act to make such decisions. The Court justified its decision by analyzing the content of the program and the situation in which the stations found themselves. In a separate opinion, concurring judges urged the unwisdom of deciding the case based upon an analysis of the factual content of the program. The concurrence was grounded upon a conclusion that it was not necessary for the Court to decide whether the program was cancelled for "legitimate reasons." The critical question is how far the First Amendment controls governmental action when the state is operating a television station. The emphasis of the concurring opinion was that the state may elect the station's mission. It can be an educational mission or it can be a cultural mission or it can be something else. The opinion emphasized the federal government's operation of the Voice of America and Radio Free Europe and also the freedom of public school teachers to express their views in the classroom. Thus the publicly owned station is not a public forum which can be forced to discuss all public issues, but it also cannot be subjected to judicial censorship each time it decides to do so or not to do so.

Seven dissenting judges took the position that by cancelling this program the government was restricting free discussion of public issues and, therefore, this was in violation of the First Amendment rights of the listeners. Note that this is the same sort of analysis as that of the dissenters in *Columbia Broadcasting System v. Democratic National Committee.* At least one judge emphasized the fact that while the decision could have been made in the first place not to broadcast the program, the decision to withdraw the program was invalid because it was based upon advocacy, or more technically, the refusal to advocate a particular viewpoint. The Supreme Court denied *certiorari* in this case. (103 S. Ct. 1274 [1983].)

If we walk a tightrope in monitoring to a degree at least the content of the broadcasting of the electronic media which is privately owned and operating for profit, we must then go on and recognize how much more difficult is walking the tightrope when the government itself is engaged in activities in the nature of the exercise of freedom of speech and press. Yet, a publicly owned and operated broadcasting station should have every right to put on a program expressing the views of various persons concerning separation of church and State, busing and racial quotas, or indeed the presidential debates themselves. After all, we certainly must discuss these matters in public schools and universities. Public broadcasting must be able to program. The limitation must be found in programming which becomes so unbalanced in its propagandizing that it runs afoul of constitutional or statutory standards. There can be no dispute—this is an exceedingly difficult line to draw.

We come to the end of a frequently travelled road. It is not always a comfortable journey. As I mentioned at the beginning, the emphasis has been upon limitations simply because that is where the issues arise. We must not overemphasize those limitations. The press and all citizens are free to express ideas, beliefs, and opinions, subject only to an imminent incitement to evils which threaten lives or national security.

With the routine acceptance of freedom of speech and press which we enforce in this country, it is difficult for us to realize how uniquely broad are our protections of the media. The British Official Secrets Act creates strong limitations upon press freedom in England. That statute prohibits a number of activities

which are "prejudicial to the safety or interests of the
state." Thus, talking with a foreign agent—anyone
hired by a foreign government to do anything in or out
of Great Britain prejudicial to the safety or interests of
the state—is a crime. On the surface this does not
sound so bad, but under the statute you need not
prove prejudice to the state; it is presumed. You can
prove it simply by proving the "known character" of
the person accused of the offense. Further, you can
prove talking with a "foreign agent" solely by proving
that you have the address of a foreign agent.

It is actually forbidden for anyone to have any picture of an atomic power plant, no improper intent
required. Further, it is improper for anyone to possess
a picture of any military installation or "property of the
Queen" with intent to prejudice the safety or interests
of the state. Under these provisions, of course, criticism of the location or operation of a military base, or
publishing a picture of such a base, or a park or power
plant, creates great risks for the press because
whether it is prejudicial or not is virtually solely in the
hands of the prosecuting authorities. The only controls
under this statute to keep it from being applied in an
extremely oppressive fashion are the assurance of high
government officials that they will not use it op-
pressively and the requirement in the statute that
prosecutions cannot be undertaken without the
approval of the Attorney General of Great Britain.

In 1975, there was a major cause celebre when an
American journalist who had worked on the *London
Evening Standard* for six years was expelled from the
country for "obtaining documents in violation of the

Official Secrets Act." He was not told and no one else was ever told what those documents were. There was never a public hearing or trial. He was not allowed to have a lawyer represent him, and he was simply expelled under the immigration laws. The press took up the battle for the journalist, but the matter was "stonewalled" at every turn by the British government.

Obviously, the government exercises substantial restraint in enforcing this statute. But the iron fist is beneath the velvet glove, and all of the press knows it and is wary of it. In a study of comparative free speech in Britain, France, and the United States I made some years ago, the two great criticisms I heard constantly repeated by the British press was first, the fear of the Official Secrets Act, and second, the strict application of the defamation laws against the press.

In this same study of comparative free speech, I interviewed a highly respected French university professor who called himself a "left-wing Gaullist." He commented upon the practice from time to time of the French government shutting down a newspaper in France when it becomes too obstreperously critical of the government in power. He asserted to me that France had the best system in the world to deal with this problem. If the newspaper got too far out of line, the government would shut it down. Then after a period of negotiations, the newspaper would agree to certain guidelines with the government and reopen. Finally, about a year later the French Conseil d'Etat would declare that the seizure of the newspaper had been illegal. This system was seriously lauded because it enabled the state to control a newspaper which was causing too much trouble and yet the law did not develop a principle that the state could do so!

You can see why I say our protections are the strongest to be found anywhere in the world. In contrast, our media are free to criticize policies and practices of the government, of private organizations, and of citizens. Ideas and opinions are unrestricted. The concept of defamation has been narrowed by the Supreme Court to relatively extreme areas of abuse.

Finally, let us remind ourselves that in the geographical areas of the globe in which well over half of the people of this world live, what I have said here could well cause me to be sent to prison. And the fact that you are here and listening would make you vulnerable to imprisonment as well. In behalf of freedom of the press, we must put up with annoyance and a good deal of rubbish. But this is not a large price to pay for liberty. Justice Robert Jackson once said: "Liberty is like electricity. There can be no substantial storage. It must be generated as it is enjoyed, or the lights go out." While we insist on a measure of balance by carefully applied limitations, the watchword is liberty.

RELIGIOUS FREEDOM AND HUMAN RIGHTS: A "PUBLIC THEOLOGICAL" PERSPECTIVE

by

Max L. Stackhouse

Max L. Stackhouse

Professor Stackhouse received a B.A. from Depauw University. After a year of study at the Nederlands Opleidings Institut in Breukelen, Holland, he earned a B.D. at the Harvard Divinity School and a Ph.D. at the Harvard Graduate School of Arts and Sciences. He is an ordained minister in the United Church of Christ.

After serving as a Lecturer in Ethics at the Harvard Divinity School for two years, Professor Stackhouse joined the faculty of the Andover Newton Theological School. He was named Professor and Chairman of the Department of Religion and Society (a joint doctoral program of Andover Newton and Boston College) in 1972. he has been a visiting professor at the United Theological College in Bangladore, India, on three separate occasions and a visiting lecturer in colleges and universities in Fiji, Singapore, Indonesia, and the Philippines.

Professor Stackhouse is past director and executive secretary of the Society of Christian Ethics; a member of the editorial boards of the Journal of Religious Ethics, Soundings, *and the* Review of Religious Research; *and a member of a number of professional associations.*

In addition to many scholarly articles, Professor Stackhouse is the author of The Ethics of Necropolis *(1971),* Ethics and the Urban Ethos *(1972), and* Creeds, Societies, and Human Rights *(1984).*

RELIGIOUS FREEDOM AND HUMAN RIGHTS: A "PUBLIC THEOLOGICAL" PERSPECTIVE

by

Max L. Stackhouse

It may be seen by some as an exaggeration to claim that freedom of religion is the most important human right and that threats to religious freedom are now threatening human rights. Nevertheless, I intend to argue that the misunderstanding of both religious freedom and human rights and the neglect of the public theological issues behind these by today's intellectual and religious leadership threaten the fabric of civilization and the tissue of moral values in a free society.

I am well aware that religious freedom does not stand at the pinnacle of much contemporary thinking about the destiny of civilization. Those who daily confront the threat of starvation and those who ponder the problem of world hunger are inclined to accept the advice of Bertolt Brecht: "First feed the face; then worry about right." Those who are daily threatened with disappearance, with torture, with rape, with troops marching through the door at night, or with systemic economic exploitations might also have reservations about the importance of religious freedom. They might well retort: "Get the exploiters off our necks, then we can talk about prayer, piety, and providence." Still further, those alert to the perils of ecological disaster prompted by population explosions amidst limited resources or to the haunting specter of nuclear exchange followed by a devastating "nuclear winter" might also wonder why we fret with such questions as religious freedom when the whole of humanity might be plunged into a new stone age or wholly destroyed. Is religious freedom not marginal to the issues of our age? How can there be human rights if there is no humanity; how can we speak of religious freedom if there is neither society nor a pervasive will to halt the madness of escalating militarization?

The concerns of such voices are not wrong. It is the sensitive consciences who grasp the scope of vicious evil in the world and who struggle against it in word and deed. These are the unsung heros and heroines of our day who have grasped a vision of the whole and are ready to pour out their lives for others. It is the barbarians and new pagans in our midst who slickly mouth pious phrases yet who have no care for the hungry neighbor, the trampled and victimized of the world, violations of the creation, the nuclear peril, human rights for all, or religious freedom for others.

And yet, the quiet heros and heroines of our day may be in error in one respect, one of great concern to me as an ecumenically and socially concerned theologian. Many of my closest colleagues and associates are today engaged in extending theological reflection and action on behalf of those who are poor and oppressed and against the systemic threats to ecological and nuclear destruction, but many see little connection between the issues to which they have given their lives and the fundamental, even overriding structural issues of religious freedom or human rights. The mistake is in part an understandable one, for both religious freedom and human rights are frequently defined in such trivial ways that it would indeed be foolish to spend much time fretting about them. For one thing, freedom of religion is often understood to entail little more than the fact that people believe all sorts of nonsense as a purely private preference and ought to be allowed to do so. Religion is viewed as an optional personal predilection which some people—particularly the prescientific and uneducated—might care to exercise, much as sophisticated people with greater aesthetic sensibility but equally irrational fixations might take up renaissance music, bird-watching, Scottish dancing, or yoga. Some people are into this, some into that, and there you are. *De gustibus non disputandum.* Freedom of religion, in this view, is readily granted, because it is seen as a purely personal matter, one properly to remain at least in the irrational recesses of consciousness and at most in family devotions or in pious gatherings under the steeple—in any case well isolated from those things that make a difference in the public world. This view is not only held by those who are fundamentally skeptical of all things religious, but also by a number of clergy and religious leaders who focus all their preaching and teaching on the irrational leap of faith which links the isolated soul to absolute transcendence and by those who engage in spiritual quests by retreat from all "merely exterior" questions. Members of both these religious groups resist drawing any connection between religion and social, political, or economic matters. Ironically, this is also the view held in those

societies which are militantly atheistic. They allow
freedom of conscience and spiritual devoutness in
matters of religion so long as it has no chance to have
any implications for social relationships and public
matters. Sadly, this is the view apparently held by at
least some of those responsible for IRS rulings about
which activities of religious groups are to be tax ex-
empt, because they are purely private and hence truly
religious, and which are not. If religious freedom is
understood in any of these ways, then religious freedom has the appearance, at least, of an esoteric concern in the face of *real* problems which are to be dealt
with politically, although historical experience suggests that wherever politics is allowed to become the
sovereign authority for all aspects of human society,
not only is religious freedom curtailed, but also the
stage is set for the systemic violation of human rights
by political authority.

The understanding of human rights is also frequently so lacking in amplitude that many can see
little connection between the call for human rights and
the great issues of hunger, exploitation, ecology, and
nuclear warfare. Most frequently, human rights are
seen to be no different than civil liberties which are
properly within the provenance of policy matters. The
difference, however, is critical. Civil liberties are
those entitlements granted, conceded, or created by a
civil order. They are instituted by regimes and governments and enforced, insofar as they are attended to
at all, by and within nation-states. Inevitably, civil
liberties grow out of specific political histories and
cultures and can be altered by modifications of that
history by the rise of power. What governments pro-

mulgate regarding civil liberties by fiat or by prescribed procedure or by constitutional guarantees can
be revoked by edict or legislation or constitutional
change. One need only to investigate the history of
civil liberties in Eastern Europe, in the Philippines, in
Black- or White-dominated African countries, or in
South Korea, Cuba, Iran, Argentina, or Nicaragua to
see what I mean.

Human rights are not of this order. Human rights
are not made by governments and cannot be repealed
by them. Human rights imply a view as to what is
universally human and what is universally right that
transcends any specific civil order or political culture,
whether they are instituted by any particular government or not. The very term "human rights" implies,
above all, that there is a universal moral order to
which all civil laws and social policies in all countries
ought to conform and on the basis of which the various
political cultures of the world can and should be evaluated. Human rights may, in fact, collide with pro-
mulgated civil liberties at certain points. I do not
mean to minimize civil liberties in the least. More
often than not they are the most effective civilizational
instrument available to protect human rights, and
those who do the most to protect civil liberties are
more often than not those who are also the greatest
protectors of human rights. This is particularly the
case in societies, like this one, where certain civil
liberties, such as that in the first Article of the Bill of
Rights, embody fundamental human rights. Nor do I
intend to slander those exciting and dramatic forma-
tions of "base communities" under the flag of some
"liberation theologies" that are taking place in parts of

Latin America and Asia. Several of these movements are engaged in creative new directions which bring new vistas of religious freedom and civil liberties to peoples and countries where they have too long been denied. However, the ideological use of Marxist and sometimes Leninist categories to interpret their social-historical situation bears within it the prospects for the destruction of just those religious freedoms and human rights they seek to establish, for the liberationist understanding of civil liberties makes them totally maleable to the "will of the people" as determined by single party regimes. There are arenas, as we shall see, where civil liberties in this definition do not adequately guard human rights.

The key problem in this regard is that reliance on civil liberties alone can go, and has gone, in one of two directions—the libertarian and the liberationist. The libertarian view (developed originally as "liberalism" but ironically now called "conservative" in America) is the view that attempts to protect the value of individual freedom above all other values. This is an important value, but it can become twisted when it is too eagerly applied to economic life where every person is motivated to maximize economic advantage by scalping the neighbor if it seems advantageous to do so, or applied without remainder to the corporation as a *persona ficta* in countries where legal and political systems provide no countervailing checks and balances. This is not the place to enter into an analysis of the various ideologies of "liberal capitalism" except to note that many of the more vigorous proponents of libertarian views have given capitalism a bad name around the world in terms of human rights. They have failed to articulate in their arguments or demonstrate in practice (especially in underdeveloped nations) the degree of cooperation, team work, sacrificial discipline, and concern for the general welfare which have made capitalist mixed economies in North Atlantic countries the most productive, successful, and, arguably, the more equitable economies of the modern world. In any case, the burden of proof is on those who tend toward the libertarian interpretation of civil liberties to show that free economic institutions cannot only engender mighty machines of individualist and consumer-oriented production for the Western sectors of the Northern Hemisphere but also can and do enhance the viability of constitutional democracy around the world, feed the hungry, defend minorities and the victimized masses of the world, utilize the resources of creation in ways that make human life sustainable for generations yet unborn, and reduce the dangers of nuclear war and militarization. If that cannot be done, the concern for civil liberties in the libertarian economic mold will be seen more and more widely, as it is many places already, as a threat to human well-being, as something that has to be overthrown in order to secure human rights. Already those who think that a modulated "capitalism with a human face" could do these things are suspect among international leaders of most of the world's religious faiths.

The latter tendency is already present in many parts of the world under the name "liberationism," as I have mentioned. In various liberation movements, the judgment against libertarian concerns, and with it historic alliances with constitutional democracy and capitalist economics, has in the main already been made. Civil liberties, in these perspectives, are seen as but the masks for bourgeois economic interests which legitimate systemic exploitation. The "human" and "right" social mandate, as liberationists speak of it, is the creation of revolutionary solidarities among the oppressed whereby the disadvantaged can wrest control over their destinies, by force if necessary, from those who now keep them in thraldom, and establish a "true" democracy where "the people" establish a collective freedom to control their future. This is not the place to discuss the various nationalist and socialist theories to which liberationist perspectives are often attached. The data of history are not yet in, but already one can see a growing skepticism about liberationism in most parts of the world where this view has become prominent. The burden of proof is on socialist lands, nationalist ideologies, and those liberationist movements operating against authoritarian regimes to demonstrate that they can develop societies which in fact protect human rights, establish democracy, and develop viable political economies. Thus far, they have not been able to do this.

The main point that I want to make at this juncture is that neither of these views has shown that it can feed the hungry neighbor, compassionately lift up the oppressed, evidence stewardly care for the ecosphere, overcome the demonic tendency toward nuclear war, *and* establish open societies. Further, what makes these two wings of the modern world so similar, for all their differences, is deep philosophical bias they share. Both hold the view that human rights are essentially a matter of an artifact created by the will of the people. (For one it arises with the mythical "social contract," for the other from a mystical "revolutionary consciousness.") Both have a view of history which understands the past and much of the present in terms of rule by the will of others—what is called "heteronomy" in philosophical jargon. Humanity, in this view, is held in servitude by *imposed* belief by some "other" power, such as feudal elites or patriarchal authorities who dominate everyone else, using arms, food, law, and religion as means of social control. Against this "heteronomy," humanity is seen to be in the process of exposing the fraud of it all, wresting control of human destiny from the gods, the priests, the princes, and the patriarchs, and forging the human future solely on the basis of our innate human wills, imagination, needs, and purposes. "Autonomy," self-rule, not heteronomy, is the ideal for persons and societies. Each individual, each nation should be sovereign in itself. It must offer resistance to any imposed order. Autonomy is the only norm—although the two wings of this tradition disagree as to whether the truly autonomous unit is to be the sovereign individual, as the libertarians say, or the paramount collectivity (the proletariat, the decolonialized nation, the race, the class, the gender), as the liberationists say. Civil rights, like religions, are a creation of the human will, a projection of our personal imaginations or our social needs. The central liberty is to be free to engage in the human construction and reconstruction of life and society as will, need, desire, and power allow. The only reason to heed these artifacts derives from their relative utility in producing more "liberty."

It is fascinating to note how these two forms of secular humanism—for that is what they are, however

much they may periodically take on the coloration or
vocabularies of faith traditions—treat the facts of widespread hunger, domination, ecological danger, and
nuclear peril. Each one attributes the threats to the
"other." The libertarian sees the newfangled col-
lectivizations of societies as but a repristination of
ancient tyrannies. The liberationist attributes the evils
of the world to the individualization of commercial
interests which produces the exploitation of the many
by the few. One claims that we must save humanity by
allowing and developing more individual freedom, initiative, and creativity; the other claims that we must
engineer a "holistic" society so that a more fully inte-
grated solidarity can save humanity from the aliena-
tion and domination which individualism entails. Both
see the salvation of the world as a human, historical,
autonomous enterprise in a constant and relentless
struggle against heteronomy (which the other
represents). Each is willing to enter alliance with authoritarian governments and use totalitarian tactics if
they also are likely to constrain or defeat the other.
Both spend precious resources in militarization, di-
verting them from other uses, to prevent the other
from gaining the upper hand. Is it not the case that
what we confront, on a worldwide scale, is a pair of
deeply established "secular salvation religions" complete with myths, rituals, evangelists, and apologists,
now threatening us all and claiming to have overcome
the pathologies of past religion? If these are the views
of religious freedom and human rights that are current
around the world, then we can leave religious freedom
as a nice legacy from the ancient pilgrims who landed
at Plymouth and celebrated on Thanksgiving Day with

gluttony and leave human rights to the platitudinous
statements of the United Nations or the idealism of
Jimmy Carter, none of which worked very well, for *the*
question is a political one of autonomous individualism
versus sovereign collectivism. (See the "Forum on
Human Rights" in the Fall 1984 issue of *Soundings*,
where several scholars from East and West make just
this point.)

But I do not believe that we can leave the matter
there. Too much is at stake. Thus, I again assert the
claim, the primary thesis of this lecture, that the most
important human right is freedom of religion. It is a
claim that presumes that human rights are of first
importance for human civilizations and that we know
that hunger, exploitation, ecological destruction, and
massive nuclear warfare are wrong precisely because
they violate fundamental and universal moral laws
which "human rights," for all the common misunderstandings of what they are about, attempt to
articulate. As already mentioned, human rights point
to a universalistic ethic which transcends any particular state of affairs in human societies. Whatever contributions the individualist or the collectivist understandings of autonomous civil liberties may have
contributed to the overcoming of certain heteronomous powers in the past, it is not at all clear that
either form of the secular religiosity which these two
versions of autonomy have engendered can provide a
sense of what ethical principles ought to guide the
exercise of liberty once it is gained. As William Sullivan, among others, has argued from a modernist
"radical" perspective, "liberalism," which has issued
in both libertarianism and liberationism, is stymied

when it comes to speaking of the reality of objective values and principles of justice or right order. They therefore repair to the category of "interests" which are determined by preference, will, and power. (*Reconstructing Public Philosophy,* U. of California Press, 1982.) Alasdair MacIntyre makes a comparable argument from a "neo-clasical" perspective (*After Virtue,* U. of Notre Dame Press, 1981), although he uses the term "emotivism" from philosophical ethics for the same sort of thing.

The problem is this: Reliance on emotivist theories of liberty which understand all morality to be a creation of humans, determined solely by the preference, will, and power of individuals or of collectivities gives us a world in which hunger, exploitation, oppression, ecological destruction, and nuclear armaments are perfectly ordinary. These are the unintended but very real barbarian legacies of libertarian and liberationist presuppositions which sadly today find their greatest defense among learned pagans in our universities. What is required to alter these is an awareness of the ground and nature of that universal moral law which transcends, governs, and becomes the pattern for the constraint and transformation of the interests, emotions, preferences, and desires by which we structure power and which, without regulation by moral law, will produce more hunger, exploitation, the rape of natural resources, and war. Human rights is the modern way of speaking about a very ancient quest for normative moral order which recognizes and embodies pluralism—beyond tyranny and anarchy.

At this point, it is critical to point out the subtle but indispensable relationship of human rights to religion.

I have elsewhere demonstrated that human rights involves a doctrine about universal human nature and what it is about human nature that is sacred, inviolable, and absolute. It is our human membership in a universal community governed by a transcendently grounded moral law. Contained in this doctrine is the claim that certain principles are true and valid for all people in all societies, under all conditions of economic, political, ethnic, and cultural life. It is wrong to murder, rape, pillage, incarcerate, vaporize, or atomize people and to deny them both the necessities of life and freedom commensurate with dignity, no matter what historic society they call home or what ideology they hold. People are to live under transcending standards for personal behavior and social relationships, and even when they do not, we are to treat them according to these standards as members of our own community. Such claims rest on a vision of reality that is unavoidably religious. Every civilization which endures is founded upon a vision of what is "really real" beyond the physical facts of life and which does not rest simply on those artifacts of philosophy or politics which are engendered out of the interest, emotions, imagination, and will of human beings. Such visions are dependent upon the great transcendental revelations or ontological discoveries of that to which humans are subject, commonly called "God," which is also the ground of our morality. We can call these visions "metaphysical-moral" or "thenomous" ones. There is, of course, considerable disagreement among the world religions regarding the character of the objective reality on which our metaphysics and our morals should rest, and we shall have to speak to this

fact of pluralism later; but for the moment let us note
that all the great religions see humanity as a pluralisti-
cally structured whole with the whole under constraints that enhance the dignity of each member.
These constraints are not arbitrarily imposed by some
heteronomous social-historical pattern, although the
world's religions also recognize that that has been the
case in many societies and that these artificial dominations must be overcome. Their common point, however, is a deeper one: If heteronomy is to be overcome, human autonomy is not sufficient. Genuine
freedom requires an order, a pattern, a fabric of
normative meaning. Autonomy for each individual
means only anarchy, chaos, and the license to mutual
exploitation. Autonomy for classes, single parties, nations, and "blocks" means not only the subjugation of
persons but the liquidation of groups who do not want
to be swallowed into a single whole. The great religions of the world address the question of what it is
that should guide the will, the desires, and the imagination of humans as we attempt to seize control of
our destinies individually or collectively. They speak,
in varous vocabularies, of "theonomy" beyond heteronomy and autonomy. They mean by this a rootedness
in a divine transcendent reality that renders order
with justice and freedom with principle and form.

Perhaps at this point it has become clear why I have
developed these remarks in the present direction and
why I took issue at the outset with the heroes and
heroines of our day as an ecumenically oriented,
socially concerned theologian. Many of my closest
friends and colleagues in my church, in my seminary,
in academic societies to which I belong, and in the

councils of churches within which I work, have managed to become libertarian and liberationist at the same time. In all questions of life-style, sexuality, and private budgets, they are libertarian; in questions of political economy and international affairs, they are liberationist. In neither arena is there pronounced evidence of a profound quest for a theonomous vision which can render a universally valid and morally binding ethic for human relations and complex civilizations. They seem, indeed, not to be concerned about the problem of order at all, and concerns of *theos* are so presented as to be beyond concerns of *nomos*. Both systematically and historically, normative views of human rights of this order appear only where key religious matters are taken as central to the formation of civilizations. Not *all* religious views are of equal import in this area, to be sure. Some religions are constitutionally tribal, caste-oriented, or so given to the celebration of ethnic or nationalistic deities that they can hardly imagine a universal moral law for all humanity any more than the secular religions of libertarian or liberationist humanism can think beyond interest, will, and power. It is only in societies which have had as one of their deep presumptions that they stand under a Godly law and purpose, that they can or will be judged by God, that the notion of the rule of law over the "will of men" developed and universal human rights beyond the arbitrary privileges of "liberty" became institutionalized. (See my *Creeds, Societies and Human Rights*, Eerdmans, 1984.)

The development of this tradition of human rights is dependent on religion in another way. Freedom of religion entails the recognition that decisive struggles for human rights are won in the minds and hearts of the people which, cumulatively and over time, can shape the social ethos in the directions of a humane civilization. Freedom of religion thus entails a certain populist confidence in the people to adhere to, to be converted to, and to discern true from false religious teaching, viable from abortive ethical advice, and decent from shoddy arguments about metaphysical-moral matters when they are properly equipped to do so by profound preaching and teaching. Religious freedom is restricted in precisely those places where the people are least trusted, and the first mark of oppression appears where the doctrine prevails that officially defined error has no rights to be heard, to make its case, to propagandize, to persuade, to evangelize, and to proselytize. There is no doubt in my mind that where there is freedom of religion, false teaching, heresy, and anathema will also occur; but there is even less doubt that where freedom of religion is restricted and controlled by coercive authority, the consequence is a lie in the soul of those who adhere to official doctrine only. A civilization becomes more divided against itself under such restrictions than where open debate is in full swing with all the risks that entails. In the last decade, the scandalous conspiracy of concerned families, legal authorities misusing the legal doctrine of "conservatorship," entrepreneurs engaging in "deprogramming," and intellectuals developing theories of "brainwashing" to control freedom of religion and prevent conversion is one of the most frightening developments to destroy human rights in our land. (See H. Richardson, *Deprogramming*, Toronto School of Theology, 1977.) This leads us to a further consideration—one which focuses on the institutional dimension of civilizations where freedom of religion and human rights are recognized.

The development of human rights was not won by philosophical arguments alone, nor by strength of religious conviction alone. These organized in specific institutions which altered the shape of civilizations. Most religions are organized around one or several of the traditional modes of social power in a society: Familial and kinship solidarities constitute one of the most important forces in civilizations. People everywhere want, first of all, to take care of their own kind, to preserve and enhance the status, power, fecundity, and influence of the gene pool to which they belong. Ancestor worship, fertility cults, sacred dynasties, and even some dimensions of nearly all marriage rites and rituals are manifestations of this. Some contemporary sociobiologists, in fact, tout this as the most profound "natural law" shaping human life. (See the debates in *Zygon*, Vol. 19, No. 2 [June 1984].) A second locus of social power is economic. Adam Smith shares with Karl Marx the absoluteness of *homo economicus*. The power of this view has been sanctified wherever human life is sacrificed to the gods of productivity, success, Fortuna, class, turf, or privilege. Still a third force is political. Everywhere knees bow to power, and all the echoes of Mars, Victory, Triumph, and Regime are also honored throughout the world. And every culture has its own poetry, art, song, and dance by which it celebrates itself, often identifying these sacred artifacts as deity itself. In all these, human membership in particular societies is utilized to deny universal principles of right and universal human membership and given "sanctified," more properly called "idolatrous," approval.

But some religions have established an organizational base independent at least in principle from these other powers. The synagogue and the church, for example, where they developed as institutionally separate from family, economy, regime, and cultural communal identity, introduced a pattern of social bonding in society which has had tremendous impact on the formation of civilization. It has meant, among other things, a distinctive kind of "social space," an arena partially dependent on, but also partially independent of, the ordinary forms of social power. In a long and extremely complex history, these frail and fragile institutions have established living communities of faith which, in varying degrees, are dedicated to the actualization of a theonomous vision which transcends the persuit of personal or collective will or the pagan, absolutist demands of kin, state, wealth, and cultural artifice.

In other words, the churches, forever claiming indisputable and God-given rights to their own existence, and perennially reasserting the basic understandings of what it means to be human and what is universally right, have not only preserved the theonomous vision on which human rights rest philosophically, but they have persistently overcome the pressures of individualistic libertarianism toward the chaos of anarchy and the tendencies of collectivistic liberationism toward the terrors of tyranny to establsh free associations of persons in community as a basis for social organization. We speak here of "free association," and the term implies an alternative definition of

liberty than is understood by either the libertarians or
the liberationists. It implies an interpretation of society as an open community of communities, with each
community consisting as an association of persons
gathered to perform specific functions and to embody
specific principles and values, under a divine reality.

This view, first worked out in theory and practice in
ecclesiology, has implications far beyond any specific
church. This definition does not presume that the
starting point for civilizational life is either the individual or the herd, but rather that both the self and
the collective are, empirically, and ought to be shaped
by the fabric and tissue of human interactions and
memberships when these enhance personal development and the common good in accord with the best
ethical principles humans can discover and voluntarily
embrace. It is for this reason that we can properly say
that individual liberties and collective freedoms (of the
state particularly, but also of the proletariat—the
masses—or of some "people") are not absolute. Communities of persons religiously bonded into voluntary,
noncoercive societies of discipline, fidelity, and service are historically, logically, and morally prior to individuals (it takes two persons to produce a new one).
Communities of fidelity, which form the context
where the one is nurtured, are prior to collectivities
(faith communities are the core of society, and society
is prior to states and can alter them). Whatever the
silliness of much that goes on in some churches, whatever the frequency of stupidity on the part of church
leaders and of pretentious self-righteousness among
believers, this institutional and civilizational dimension of religion is of inestimable importance for the

history and understanding of human rights, and it is
the right to form such associations against accepted
patterns of familial, governmental, economic, and
cultural power that constitutes the fundamental meaning of religious freedom.

In the long course of history, this much neglected
institutional dimension of religion has had a major
impact. The traditionally sacred and absolute authority of the tribe, of the regime, of wealth, and of cultural form has been relativized. They continue still, of
course, to have considerable force. Racism, the legacy
of attaching sacred status to one or another clan, tribe,
caste, or gene pool, is not overcome in fact, although it
is morally and spiritually overcome in principle. At
more personal levels, nepotism and corruption for the
sake of "my" family's security remain scandals. The
proper regard for patriotism, for loyalty to one's nation, is another area which often treds a thin line in the
direction of idolatry. But all morally sensitive believers feel that something is awry when the Soviets speak
of their "sacred" air space when they shoot down a
Korean airliner, and just as awkward when Americans
so identify holiness and Americanism that they can no
longer be critical of moral defect at home. That many
seem to be motivated by greed and lust for gain can
hardly be denied; but that wealth is proof of virtue and
righteousness is flatly denied by novelists, dramatists,
poets, ethicists, and preachers as well as by business
leaders and union members throughout this wealthiest
of societies. And so one could go on. The main point is
that the final legitimacy of all the "natural" institutions
of social power can be compromised, limited, and

modulated by the freely organized religious associations, and that religious groups have an inalienable
right to exist and specifically to attempt the noncoercive transformation of these institutions by preaching,
teaching, persuasion, experiment, and example.

The social space defined, defended, and expanded
by the churches over the centuries has now broadened
to allow a wider range of "voluntary associations."
Dissent committees, charitable associations, professional organizations, independent presses, labor
organizations, service clubs, interest groups, multiple
political parties and action committees, and a vast
array of what sociologists call "intermediary institutions" and what the United Nations calls "non-
governmental organizations" are characteristic of
those societies where religious freedom has had a
chance to work its influence and engender pluralistic,
open societies with a social context supportive of persons and a limited state. It is likely that we cannot see
the import of this, for it has become so much a part of
our social environment that it seems the natural way to
live. Yet when we visit or study societies where this
institutional dimension has not been worked out and
institutionalized in law (which is most societies in most
of the world throughout human history), we can see
how rare and precious it is. Religious freedom in this
sense is the *social* foundation of human rights, just as
the notion of a universal moral law rooted in a
theonomous reality beyond the practicalities of the
empirical world is the *ideational* foundation. The new
barbarians of our day, however, have no comprehen-
sion of this and are ready to relinquish the heritage by

neglecting both this fabric of sociality and the import of those visions on which pluralistic, constitutional societies, which protect human rights, exist.

Is it not the case that when we want to do something about hunger, about exploitation, about ecological disruption, or about nuclear war, we organize committees to raise these issues, to preach and teach about them, and to alter public policy where it causes these? Do we not properly claim the absolute, God-given right to do so? Do we not find that the greatest support we get for these issues comes directly from those deeply dedicated to the freedom of religion, to human rights, and to the preservation and extension of a pluralistic society ruled by law, to those, in short, who have caught the vision, however inarticulately? Even should we decide that the most important questions have to be addressed politically, let us note that the Constitution of the United States, or of any other democratic land affected by these traditions, does not provide for the establishment of particular political parties. Yet, the voluntary organization of political parties and movements has a presumption of immunity from governmental control or, for that matter, from absolute familial control, control by a commercial interest, or control by a single cultural form. To be sure, groups must obey the general criminal, health, and safety codes of the whole society, but the doctrines they teach, the structures of authority they develop internally, and whether they are for or against the present organized structure of family, regime, economy, or culture are presumptively outside governmental control.

Laurence Tribe, the noted constitutional lawyer, puts it this way: "If one believes . . . that legitimate power is delegated to the state by individuals and groups, and that certain groups under our constitutional scheme have never relinquished their private authority . . . as centers of deeply shared experience and faith, then religious institutions emerge not as repositories of unaccountable, delegated state power, but as irreducible components of our social order, secure against all but the most limited and most compellingly justified forms of government intervention." (See D.M. Kelley, Ed., *Government Intervention in Religious Affairs*, Pilgrim Press, 1981, p. 32.) He goes on to show that freedom of the press and of charitable and political organizations have similar immunities with similar roots, and had his topic been broader, he could have added familial, economic, or cultural power to his phrase about the State. The belief and the constitutional scheme to which he refers derive from the intertwined history of religious freedom and human rights which is the most important structural legacy of modern democracy.

Today we face what appear to be new perils to the whole question of human rights and religious freedom. The perils not only come from repristinated and oddly combined forms of libertarianism and liberationism, now frequently baptized into the fundamentalisms of the right and the left and poised to make older controversies between religious conservatives and religious liberals look like child's play, but also from a wide range of perilous issues for all religious parties for which neither theology or society is prepared. Some of the scope of this set of issues is reflected in the fact that there are some 7000 ongoing lawsuits involving churches at this time, with nearly 4000 of them involving human rights and religious liberties questions. Other dimensions of our present peril can be seen in highly publicized cases such as the one when a small, religiously communitarian sect in Vermont is raided in the night by state troopers and more than a hundred children are taken into custody because of reputed, but unproven, possibilities of child abuse. Or the incarceration of Reverend Moon, head of the Unification Church (commonly called the "Moonies"), for following practices fully in accord with his community's principles of theology and polity—over the protests of groups ranging from the National Council of Churches, the American Civil Liberties Union, the (evangelical) Christian Legal Society, and numerous Catholic, Jewish, Fundamentalist, and humanist leaders, none of whom agree with Reverend Moon's theology or polity. One could also mention the case of Bob Jones University or the Faith Baptist Church case in Nebraska. If one adds to this brief list the questions of religious influences on public policy regarding abortion, family life, pornography, and homosexuality as well as the National and World Councils of Churches' and the Roman Catholic Bishops' statements about nuclear war, on economic life, against racism, and on the status of women, to cite just some widely known examples, we can see that a wide range of questions about religion and public life is present everywhere. While some political leaders, many members of the press, and many in the general population display their ignorance about religious freedom, human rights, and constitutional guarantees by decrying the undue involvement of religion in social and political questions, the decisive issue may well be precisely the opposite—the intrusion of government into religious matters.

It is important that we listen to specialists who know the details of constitutional law when addressing these matters. But some of the debates involve proposals to change the constitution and hence become issues of a fundamental ethical kind—what principles shall guide us at this transconstitutional level? The task of a theological educator concerned with social and ethical questions is to address these matters in a rather particular way. And the chief concern that I have on these questions at this time is the simple fact of overwhelming ignorance about them. The ignorance is due, I think, to three factors: an educational failure, a theological failure, and a pastoral failure. In other words, it is a failure of three communities to which I belong and to which I have given my life. Let me treat each of them briefly.

I warrant that it is not stretching the matter too far to say that most college graduates, including those with graduate degrees, are somewhere around grade school level on the average when it comes to understanding the role that religion plays in social history and the formation of civilizations around the world in the past and in the present. The problem is compounded by the fact that the stated policy of most public schools is to stand clear of religion, as if religion ever has been or ever could be isolated from questions of science, literature, music, psychology, law, anthropology, philosophy, politics, and economics. In

part, this is due to the tragic misunderstandings between science and religion since Galileo, still only
partly repaired, the general influence of the
Enlightenment (which saw all religion as "heteronomy") on the structures of education in the West,
and the more recent influence of John Dewey's
pragmatism—particularly in the schools of education
in America. In addition, there is the realistic recognition among school administrators that it could easily
become the zealots of one or another religion who
would most like to get their hands on a religion course
and use the patterns of school discipline and state
authority behind public schools to proselytize, to shift
from learning about religion (which is permitted) to
indoctrination in or practice of a specific religion
(which is not legally allowed). Whatever the causes,
the United States could be said to have the highest
density of well-educated, highly trained, religiously
illiterate populations in the world outside the Eastern
bloc nations. This phenomenon is occurring precisely
at the moment when new encounters with the world's
religions are made more and more frequent due to the
technological, commercial, communications, and
travel opportunities these well-trained people have
introduced. It is occurring also just as "media minis-
tries" and computerized membership and contribution techniques make visible minority religious perspectives which present doctrines incomprehensible
to today's *literati,* and just as grass roots people find
their relatives or friends of friends, starved for spiritual and metaphysical-moral depth, converted to the
Jews for Jesus, Black Islam, the Divine Light Mission,
Hare Krishna, the Worldwide Church of God, Sufi,

some local sect, or for that matter to the Roman Catholic, Presbyterian, Southern Baptist, or Unitarian churches. In more cases than not the public educational institutions of our land have simply not prepared the population to know what is happening to them. The neglect and avoidance of religion because it seemed wrongheaded to some, irrelevant to others, and likely to induce conflict to still others, means that large segments of the American intelligentsia simply do not know how to deal with its force in human affairs. That is one source of the modern temptation to a new barbarism.

Even more troubling, in this regard, many educators do not seem to hold that it is possible to make scholarly judgments about the relative moral, intellectual, sociopolitical, and philosophical worth of different religious traditions. One of my colleagues likes to quote Paul Valery's famous article of 1919, "la crise de l'esprit," to the effect that Western civilization has renounced all standards of judgment in religion, philosophy, and morals and is at a loss to demonstrate that truth should prevail over error because it has finally decided that the distinction between them is unclear. His judgment may well be a much too strong indictment of the whole civilization, but it may have direct implications for the ways in which religion is handled, where it is at all, in public education. One must be cautious about painting too bleak a picture here, for there are scholars active in seminaries, departments of religion, the American Academy of Religion, the Society for the Scientific Study of Religion, the Institute on Religion in an Age of Science, and comparable organizations who are working vigorously

at just these questions. Nevertheless, the evidence
that the fruit of their labor has had any penetrating
impact on the structures of education for the whole
population is slight indeed. In consequence, we confront not a discerning population able to judge the
relative adequacy of the differences in doctrines between Billy Graham and Harvey Cox, Catholics and
Orthodox, Methodists and Mennonites, Quakers and
Calvinists, Sunni and Sufi, Zen and B'hai except that,
like pieces of modern art, they are attracted to some
and disgusted with others. We have a functional
polytheism in which every faith is treated as equal and
equally irrelevant to the truth of matters historical,
cultural, scientific, and social because it appears to be
all a matter of upbringing and preference.

Now from one perspective, that is as it should be.
That one perspective is that the public schools are, at
least partially, instruments of the government, and as
government a school may not become the adjudicator
in matters religious. It is not competent to do so. But
public schools and colleges are not, and dare not become, in my judgment, mere instruments of the State
in a way that makes governmental neutrality the occa-
sion of educationl and academic ignorance and neglect
of just those matters critical for learning. Schools are
also subject to standards of academic excellence, intellectual honesty, and the cultivation of full-orbed,
critical understandings of life and culture in ways that
governmental agencies are not. State supported educational institutions have the right, both constitutionally and under human rights, to academic
freedom. And they have the duty, under the mandates
of professional responsibility and a quest for truth, to

prepare the next generation for responsible world citizenship, to treat religious matters with all the scholarly and scientific rigor they give to biology, sociology, and geography. In fact, these and related subjects are surely not well understood until the relationship of religion to each of them is articulated, examined, and cross-examined. To be sure, there are many who doubt that this can be done, in any sense, "objectively." But that is just the point. If it is claimed that social, political, scientific, historical, and economic opinions and hypotheses can be taught and examined "objectively" but moral, spiritual, and religious matters cannot, educators have imposed an ideological judgment on religion—as something not amenable to analysis as a truth claim, as something in which it is impossible to err, as something totally irrational, as something dispensable to intellectual and cultural understanding, as something irrelevant to mature and "holistic" development. This judgment is unwarranted and flatly denied by all religions and most serious scholarship. In making their judgment, educators simultaneously assert that other things they do teach are of an entirely different order and both can be and are taught "objectively," the evidence for which is scandalously slender. Such judgments suggest that either Paul Valery's judgment about the crisis of Western Civilization or the evangelicals of our day who fear the establishment of "secular humanism" as the official religion of the public schools are more correct than I believe to be the case.

Three remedies to this situation have been proposed. One is of longstanding, and I think we shall see it extended and institutionalized on a much wider level in the years to come: That is the right to have alternative schools to public ones. Parochial schools, private schools, and various academies are not only allowed for those who are convinced that proper education involves direct treatment of religious and ethical values of a specific kind, but where religious worship and indoctrination is practiced as a part of the curriculum. While critical issues of racial and economic justice are sometimes presented by these institutions, I expect to see them expand so long as the educational confusion about religion continues in public education. At present, some 1000 such schools, or about three per day, are being formed each year. Indeed, we can expect increased pressure for something like the "voucher" system whereby each child is allotted so much public money to utilize as he and his parents see fit in a parochial, a private, *or* a public school. This prospect is, in my judgment, both salutary, in that it will force all educators to think more clearly about the role of religion in the educational enterprise, and frightening, in that it sets the stage for difficult battles about what standards shall be applied by government agencies for accreditation of such nonpublic schools where such vouchers can be used.

A second solution to the problem of religion and education is the cry for the institutionalization of prayer or meditation as a regular part of the public school day. Here, I think, the religious and political advocates of the practice are just plain wrong on every ground—constitutionally, practically, and in terms of religious liberty and human rights. As was said at the Senate Judiciary Committee's Subcommittee on the Constitution June 26, 1984, "Whenever civil authority seeks—at one and the same time—to don the sanctifying cloak of religious ceremony to wield the supreme authority [of the State] to tailor religious destiny, then both the denial of religious freedom and the danger of political opression are gravely realized." *(The Religious Freedom Record* [Summer 1984], p. 9.) More important for me, they are theologically wrong. As I argued earlier, the genius of religious freedom as the decisive basis for human rights is that it allows, even demands, "free association." Forced prayer or required moments for meditation with the weight of state coercion behind it is the first step toward an imposed spiritual lie in the souls of persons and the body politic as a whole.

The advocates of prayer in the public schools have, however, one point in their favor. They are alert to the fact, as only the very best teachers also are, that learning, teaching, study, and discussion in all areas of academic concern are best conducted in an arena where one thinks and reflects and examines with an attitude of reverence toward truth and the source of truth, which is larger and deeper and wider than the specific topic under consideration. All the various disciplines perceptively pursued require a sensitivity to "metaphysical-moral" reality that is finally unavoidable. But that reality is unlikely to be induced by the prescribed moment of prayer and can be more appropriately acknowledged by competent and profound teaching and learning and by solid instruction in what is at stake in the phenomenon of religion.

The third, most recent, proposal to deal with the relative vacuum on religious matters in public education is the newly passed law allowing religious, as well

as political and philosophical, groups to have equal
access to school facilities before and after school hours.
It provides that all meetings must be voluntary and
that school employees who oversee the meetings must
oversee the proceedings in a "nonparticipating" way.
In spite of strong fears among religious leaders with
whom I usually agree (see J.M. Wall, "New Right
Wins Equal-Access Fight," *Christian Century* [Aug.
1, 1984], p. 732), I think this is a fundamental gain for
religious liberty and human rights. If all sorts of other
clubs, groups, and organizations structured around
value commitments are permitted access, why should
not faith communities be allowed? This new legislation
seems to be fully in accord with the fabric of voluntary
associational, pluralistic democracy which is one of the
chief fruits of religious liberty and human rights. To be
sure, one can expect a number of controversies to
derive from this decision, for it is likely that the most
militant, fundamentalist, and fanatical sects and cults
will be the most eager to exploit this new opportunity,
and they may be already gearing up to pour time,
money, and effort into the mobilization of high school
students to meet in their natural habitat. Still, there is
no reason why other religious groups cannot do the
same, why the doctrines and practices of these groups
cannot and should not be subject to careful academic
scrutiny as a part of the academic study of religion, and
why these groups should be denied what is permitted
to, say, the Jefferson-Jackson Society, a profeminist
club, 4-H, Y-Teen, antinuclear groups, or the Shakespeare club. The fact that religious groups might enact
their values by prayer, singing, chant, or study of the
Bible, the Koran, or the Gita, or try to get others to

join does not substantively disqualify their right to meet since the other groups enact their own core values in ways that are surely not uncomparable. Further, the necessity of deciding, and of determining the principles for deciding, whether to participate in a particular religious voluntary association and what difference it makes in giving meaning to life is surely an activity which prepares the student for life and which is amenable to church and parental influence wherever these are strong and responsible.

Earlier I mentioned that the present ignorance of religious matters in our society which threatens religious freedom and human rights is due to educational failure, theological failure, and pastoral failure. I turn now to the second of these. Sadly, many of the things that can be said of public education can also be said of contemporary theology. Much theology, these days, has become merely confessional. That is, it is little more than the rationalization of one or another idiosyncratic religious position and does not presume that we can evaluate the relative worth of competing religious stances. In a time of religious confusion, confessionalism does play an important role. It serves to clarify distinctive teachings of a specific denomination for those who are faithful but ignorant adherents and to allow nonadherents to see what a group stands for. But confessionalism has difficulty in stating why anyone not already a part of the confessing group should heed its precepts and makes it appear that any pronouncements on public issues are simply the imposition of a privileged, unwarranted position. (See R.W. Lovin, *Christian Faith and Public Choice*, Fortress, 1984.) In contrast to "mere confessionalism," a

number of scholars are attempting to clarify what
might be entailed in a "public theology." (See, for
instance, the *fora* on this topic in *This World* [Spring
1984], Issue 8; and in *Word and World* [Summer
1984], Vol. IV, No. 3.)

A Public Theology recognizes that some dimensions
of faith are properly "private"; they involve dimensions of the soul's intercourse with God, for example, which are both highly personal and inextric-
ably woven into the fabric of symbolic language and
ritual practice to which particular confessional groups
have access on a privileged basis. But Public Theology
also attempts to identify those universal criteria and
the warrants for them by which various confessional
traditions can be evaluated whenever they presume to
guide public behavior, influence public policy, or
shape public discourse on social and ethical matters.
In addition, Public Theology holds that humans can
reliably know something about God, that careful
attention to the structure and dynamics of the decisive
touchstones of spiritual and moral authority (Scripture, Traditions, Reason, and Experience) can allow
adjudication between religious confessions about God,
that not all religions are of equal weight in terms of
their capacity to contribute to public discourse, and
that a valid theological stance will morally require
responsibility in and for the common life. In the West,
this is the tradition forged first by the confluence of
Hebraic faith and Greek philosophy and present in
various degrees and modulating forms in the thought
of Augustine, Thomas, Calvin, Wesley, Locke, Ed-
wards, Jacques Maritain, John Countney Murray, the
Niebuhrs, Martin Luther King, and others. It is a

tradition which is neglected today and which desperately needs to be revived, in new terms appropriate to our present dilemmas, if religious freedom and human rights are to be carried into the future. Finally, the kind of theology of which I now speak is willing and eager to enter the general marketplace of ideas and to develop its arguments in public arenas—not as dogmatically delivered final dicta but as nuanced dialogue, examined claim, and sustained inquiry with and among the people (and between the religions) to determine what, in fact, is universally and demonstrably true about the ultimate source and content of valid faith and ethics in cultural, social, political, and economic affairs.

It perhaps should be made clear, in this connection, that the plea for a Public Theology does not mean that theologians should run the government or dictate political policy or that we should put Christ in the Constitution. To the contrary, a Public Theology does not first think of politics, government, or regime when it uses the word "public." It thinks of the people and of society, which together shape government. It is, in fact, my conviction that professional theologians and ordained clergy who are committed to the development of a Public Theology should resign their ordination if they are elected or appointed to political office. It is *not* nonsense for the Vatican to pressure the clergy of Nicaragua's Sandinista government to decide whether their primary center of loyalty is the church or the State. Both are related to and in some ways responsible for society, but the core locus of theological authority is at stake. Public Theology may and often does take the religious and moral dimensions of political issues as its point of departure in analysis, argument, protest, or endorsement; but it operates by the power of "the word"—the pen, persuasion, and example—rather than by the direct accumulation and exercise of coercive power, which is the vocation of political and police, military, judicial, and legislative authority. Theological leadership has a more fundamental obligation to shape public opinion, social practice, and the common ethos on public matters prior to their translation into governmental polity or policy. At the most recent annual convention of the American Bar Association, Joseph Cardinal Bernadin, recently chair of the committee which drafted the U.S. Roman Catholic Bishops' statement on nuclear war, put the matter quite clearly: "The purpose of the separation of church and state in American society is not to exclude the voice of religion from public debate, but to provide the context of religious freedom where the insights of each religious tradition can be set forth *and tested.* . . . The place of the church is separate from the state but must never be separate from society. [Emphasis added.]" (United Press International reports, August 4, 1984.) To put it another way, a Public Theology attempts to clarify and gain public acknowledgment of fundamental theonomous principles by informing and persuading the hearts and minds of the people and building up normative patterns within the social ethos, but it never seeks to become theocratic. If it finds its way into governmental policy, it must be through the careful and often tediously slow formation of the conscience, convictions, agreements, and patterns of the common life and not by a religiously inspired *coup d'etat.* The first task of a Public Theology, thus, is to help the public develop the capacity to discern the difference between decent religiously rooted positions and indecent ones and to inspire them to enact the former.

This problem appears whenever theologians earnestly examine what is required to make a valid and viable statement about public matters. It also occurs when we confront, as we do in this society, a wide variety of religious postures which, episodically, "go public." What should be our response, and how might we know how to respond, when President Reagan or Governor Cuomo, Black Muslim leader Louis Farrakhan or Rabbi Balfour Brickner, Reverend Jesse Jackson or Reverend Jerry Falwell, the Caribbean Conference of Churches or the Patriarchate of Moscow make religiously grounded pronouncements, as they all have in the last year, about the morality of U.S. public policy? Especially if we do not belong to their constituencies? Are any of them true? Are some more true than others? Can we tell the difference? A Public Theology is particularly concerned with the identification of these principles and the warrants for them for assessing these religious claims and with the equipping of the population with sufficient knowledge of these principles and warrants so that the difference between serious and trivial, valid and phony truth claims about religion and morality in these various statements can be seen by the general population. Contemporary theology has been focused in one of two directions. One is called "confessionalism" or "fideism." That is, it sees theology as a thematizing of particular faiths without giving the warrant for why they should be believed in the first place. Or it has focused on critical examinations of various scholarly hypotheses set forth within very narrow technical perimeters more than it has addressed these more fundamental questions. And when a good number of contemporary theologians do address present social issues, in an attempt to be "prophetic," they seem to think that dramatic appeals for vigorous action to overcome racism, sexism, and classism, to prevent another Viet Nam in Central America, to enact the freeze, or to get the multinational corporations out of South Africa are enough. They neglect the slow, less grandiose, but perhaps more fateful and faithful work of patiently and carefully clarifying the principles and the warrants for them by which the people can make their own morally informed and theologically grounded judgments about just such public matters. I include myself and most of my professional colleagues in this indictment.

But perhaps more culpable than the professional theological community is the local clergy. In the issues under consideration here today, we are also confronted with a pastoral failure. Most people are not theologically trained, and most people do not look to the universities or even to the high schools for the fundamental values which shape their lives. Indeed, for most people, school is in the past and remembered as only slightly more than a failure, and the level of discourse in theology seems quite removed from anything having to do with real life. If there is any institution beyond the family, the mass media, the circle of immediate friends and workmates, and nationalism that shapes fundamental values and attitudes toward life, it is the local church. While local clergy may not have the prestige that they had at moments in past history, they are generally acknowledged to be the best trained and most dedicated moral authority immediately available. The problem is that many clergy are least competent in precisely the areas under discussion here.

Sadly, many of the most gifted clergy have followed the lead of modern public education, or of "confessional" fideist theology, or of the attempt to be "prophetic" by being radical. That is, they isolate their faith from questions of science, literature, anthropology, philosophy, law, politics, economics, and interreligious and cross cultural understanding; or they focus almost entirely on privileged confessional matters in attempts to induce a personal or denominational loyalty; or, if they do see the demands of faith to speak on public issues, they cover their relative incompetence by mistaking prophetic utterance for a "radicaler than thou" thunder, beating the little gatherings of faithful believers over the head for the sins of the world's betrayals of righteousness and civilization. The predictable failures of these strategies have, of course, led to a great number of crises of vocation among today's clergy—especially among those socially concerned pastors of the ecumenically oriented churches. They do not know whether they have anything much to say, theologically, and turn to various forms of "spirituality" or to psychological or sociological or managerial models of meaning to comprehend what they experience in church and society. The consequence is a failure of profound preaching and teaching among the people about the first principles of religious and ethical matters from those pastors who by virtue of the traditions they represent ought to be best suited for what is required.

It is in this context that we see, presently, the rise of absolutist and unecumenical fanaticisms, right wing and left wing, as well as numerous new cults, which provide confident certainties, without warrant or examination, among segments of the population neglected by the clergy to whom I refer. These represent a crude paganism in contrast to the sophisticated barbarians of the modern secular university. Should these new movements gain predominant influence, it would destroy human rights and religious liberty. But to be against the new barbarians and new pagans is not enough. Church leadership has also to be *for* something important. The ecumenically oriented clergy of evangelical, Roman Catholic, and "main line" backgrounds must surely take up Public Theology at the grass roots level as the main focus of preaching and adult religious education if they are to be what they have been in the past—the faithful nurturers of the humane conscience of civilization. This means, for example, they must be able to demonstrate in direct, accessible terms why Reverend Moon's doctrines should be judged as false by young people attracted to them *and* why his disciples ought to be able to propagate those views freely nevertheless. In his view, the sanctifying order for the world is his messianic family. Alienated and hurt people do need to attend to the importance and sacredness of family life, but no familial institution—even if we call it the Unification Church—can carry the full weight of theonomous responsibility. Clergy must be able to discern, and help the people to discern, why the quasi-liberationist teachings of the James Jones of the world are fatefully dangerous *before* Jonestowns happen and to give the people drawn into churches like his something better to go on. No agrarian community disciplined by one charismatic leader of doubtful character can save persons or society *in toto* as he pretended he could. Clergy must help the people at the grass roots to see why some doctrines of scriptural inerrancy as presently propagaged among some Baptists in Texas are contrary to a scriptural understanding of the authority of Scripture and turn proper Christian regard for the Bible into an Islamicized view of the Word of God, and that an enforced creedalism on this point is fundamentally contrary to both Baptistic faith and to the human rights and freedom of religion for which Baptists have long fought. They must help the people recognize why, as Catholics and Evangelicals today argue, the unmitigated and wanton destruction of potential persons by arbitrary abortions is a moral threat to human rights of staggering proportions and why the absolute forbidding of all abortion by governmental regulation is also a threat to human rights. State intrusion into the familial, medical, and psychoeconomic decisions people have to make is not likely to prevent sin and it may increase criminality. Clergy must be able and willing to show that "Transcendental Meditation" is not simply a technique for controlling one's nerves, but a metaphysical-moral vision which is Hindu through and through, and what difference it makes religiously and socially if that vision is followed. Clergy must let the people see that several of the brands of the liberation movement that are gaining so much attention in ecumenical circles today are little more than nineteenth century sociological theory only thinly sicklied over with religious jargon, while other branches of it may well be the tongue of fire of the Holy Spirit in our midst. And they must preach and teach these things, letting them filter through the conscience of the people to responsible citizenship, using democratic procedures, while defending the human rights and religious freedom of those who hold false positions.

In brief, using all the exegetical, historical, philosophical, and hermeneutical resources available to contemporary theology and employing them in the direct cultivation of the capacity of the people to make principled and warranted judgments about theological matters, the local clergy have a vocation and a mission indispensable for a true and grounded faith, for religious freedom, for human rights, and hence for the destiny of civilization which they are today only ambiguously fulfilling—a fact that forces us also to consider modifications of the educational and theological structures by which we prepare leadership for pastoral ministry.

Religion is an explosive and powerful force. And it is not always benign. If religious and educational leadership proves unable to engage the people at these levels and is unable to deprive morally pathological religious groups of their constituencies, their financial base, and their legitimacy by word, example, persuasion, conversion, analysis, and dialogue, religious freedom could produce, as it has in moments past, such pathological forms of religious fanaticism, hate, and division that political authority with the support of larger and larger majorities of the population will feel compelled to intervene to preserve the society. Already, and quite prematurely, authorities ranging from local sheriffs to the IRS are called upon to "do something" about heterodox or strange groups which are seldom challenged on theological, moral, and spiritual grounds by competent religious leadership working directly with and among the people. Human rights are the first victim of the consequent violations of religious freedom. All the perils of inquisition and witch-hunting, of religious harassment and coerced belief raise their ugly head. Proper anxiety about the prospect of these should not cause clergy to refrain from the judgment and critical evaluation of the beliefs of others but spur them to engage in just these tasks in public, without coercion, and with all the vigor they can muster. Religious freedom does not mean the absence of religious controversy; but the unending confrontation of claim with claim in the confidence that truth, righteousness, and fidelity can best find their way by the courageous, noncoercive, and relentless exposure of falsehood, evil, and fraud.

For those of you who are inclined to categorize every speech, presentation, or writing on the single spectrum between liberal and conservative, I hope you are thoroughly confused. The issues involved in religious freedom, in human rights, and in Public Theology, and which are deteriminative for both valid faith and the destiny of moral values in a free society, simply explode that simplistic dichotomy. The position here presented is profoundly liberal if one means by that the desire to preserve freedom of religion and the willingness to test religious claim by the use of human reason and experience as well as by Scripture

and tradition. The position is simultaneously profoundly conservative if one means by that it intends to
preserve and revive certain legacies of the past—
expecially those forms of theology, ethics, and a constitutional democracy under the rule of the kind of law
which is ultimately rooted in God. My greatest fear is
that the religious confusion which this land, and hence
much of the "free world," faces will induce a situation
in which the center cannot hold. As an ordained minister who is also a theological educator, I put the burden
of repairing our present malaise squarely on those
with whom I am most constantly associated—the educators, the theologians, and the church leadership,
especially at the local level, who are today not clearly
and vigorously enough attending to their precious and
sacred tasks.

ACADEMIC FREEDOM
AND RESPONSIBILITY:
MORAL VALUES ON THE CAMPUS

by

Arvo Van Alstyne

Arvo Van Alstyne

Dr. Van Alstyne served as Utah Commissioner of Higher Education and Chief Executive Officer of the Utah State Board of Regents, as well as Professor of Law at the University of Utah.

Commissioner Van Alstyne's most recent previous service was as Vice President-Executive Assistant to the President of the University of Utah (1975-1981), and as Executive Assistant to the President (1973-1975). He had been a Professor of Law at the University of Utah since 1966, coming to that position from the University of California at Los Angeles, where he served as Professor of Law from 1953 to 1966. In addition, he was a visiting Professor of Law at Stanford University and at summer sessions at Ohio State University, University of Texas, Washington University (St. Louis), and Lewis and Clark University.

Dr. Van Alstyne maintained his professional interests in the field of law by participating as a lecturer at the annual academy of American and International Law in Dallas, Texas; short courses of The Southwestern Legal Foundation in Dallas; and statewide lecture series of the California Continuing Education of the Bar.

Dr. Van Alstyne was the author of major volumes on constitutional law, state and local government law, and government tort liability, which are widely used as textbooks in law schools and by practicing attorneys.

He received the B.A. from Yale University and J.D. from Yale Law School, and was awarded an honorary LL.D. by the University of Utah in June 1984.

Arvo Van Alstyne died in January 1985, less than two months after participating in the 1984 Lectures on Moral Values in a Free Society.

ACADEMIC FREEDOM AND RESPONSIBILITY: MORAL VALUES ON THE CAMPUS

by

Arvo Van Alstyne

The widespread campus disorders which character-ized the American higher education environment in the late 1960s and early 1970s spawned (among other consequences) renewed, but by no means novel, poli-tical demands for major structural changes in tradi-tional practices of colleges and universities. In many quarters, perceptions that student unrest was to a substantial degree either fomented or encouraged by members of institutional faculties directed public attention once again to the system of faculty tenure and nurtured insistent demands for abolition or at least major reform of that system. (See generally B.L. Smith, Ed., *The Tenure Debate,* Jossey-Bass, Inc., 1973.) The critics of tenure either explicitly contended or implicitly assumed, not without justification, that the practices of academic tenure discouraged if they did not prevent the recruitment, effective discipline, or dismissal of errant professors whose conduct or expressed views had demonstrated their unfitness for fellowship in the community of scholars.

The course of the national debate on tenure, which was characterized by reports from numerous study commissions and even more numerous position pa-

pers, need not detain us here. Suffice it to say, the
outcome was an uneasy victory for the principle of
tenure, which emerged essentially intact, although
with implicit commitments to reform. Significant
modifications in current tenure practices were in fact
adopted at many institutions. Faculty selection, promotion, and tenure review procedures were strength-
ened, codes of faculty conduct were approved, tenure
management programs designed to prevent excessive
"tenuring-in" were initiated, processes for posttenure
review of faculty performance were introduced, and
generally more rigorous criteria for awarding tenure
were enacted by joint action of faculties and governing
boards. The essential principle of academic tenure,
however, survived. That principle, briefly summa-
rized, is that after successfully demonstrating his or
her qualifications for full acceptance into the community of scholars during a probationary period of suit-
able length (ordinarily seven years), the tenured faculty member is protected against termination of his or
her appointment except upon a showing of good cause,
for which the institution bears the burden of proof in
an appropriate setting of academic due process.

How can this remarkable result be explained?
While many other factors undoubtedly made a contribution, I submit that a critical element was the
virtual unanimity with which even the harshest critics
of tenure ultimately conceded its essentiality to the
preservation of academic freedom and the key role
which academic freedom plays in asuring fulfillment of
the fundamental moral obligations of higher education. The higher education community, in the whole,
wisely chose not to defend tenure primarily as a means

for assuring fair employment practices in higher education or as a system calculated to improve the economic attractiveness of the teaching profession and thereby offset the relatively meager financial rewards of career service. While these objectives have often been advanced in the past as justifying considerations, and tenure even today is widely viewed as a symbol of employment security, their basic weakness was and is obvious. It is impossible to argue persuasively that fair employment practices and academic career attractiveness cannot be assured by reasonable means other than tenure.

The primary defense of the academic tenure system, therefore, was based upon the fundamental oral imperatives which lie at the center of the higher education enterprise. In brief summary, the argument advanced three interdependent propositions:

(1) Colleges and universities are estalished to serve the common good, not only through occupational and professional career preparation, but more importantly by discharge of a pervasive moral responsibility. Through teaching, example, research, and scholarship, the university is charged by common understanding, and often by law or charter, with the profound mission to lead successive generations of students to an understanding of cultural values, advance the frontiers of knowledge, cultivate reasoning capacity, develop critical analytical skills, and nurture the means for responsible reform of social institutions based upon stable standards of critical moral judgment.

(2) The effective discharge of this fundamental

mission requires the fullest possible protection for the freedom of teachers, researchers, scholars, and students to pursue the truth in a responsible manner and to disseminate their findings and conclusions in the course of their academic duties without fear of internal or external restraints or sanctions.

(3) The theory and practice of academic tenure embody an effective, if not the only conceivable, means for protecting academic freedom.

These are powerful arguments, and they carried the field. The broad language by which they were generally articulated, however, introduced elements of ambiguity into the meaning of academic freedom which have continued to be troublesome to the present day.

One source of ambiguity is the tendency to characterize academic freedom as a particular manifestation of the more general concept of intellectual freedom safeguarded by the First Amendment. For example, the statement on "Academic Freedom and Responsibility" adopted at the Eleventh Annual Meeting of the American Association of State Colleges and Universities on November 9, 1971, proclaimed:

"The freedoms granted by the First Amendment to the Constitution of the United States are indispensable to a democratic society. Within the academic community, the vigorous exercise of these freedoms by its members—to participate in the democratic process of government as citizens, to learn and to teach what scholarship suggests is the truth, to question even what is believed to have been settled, to publish without fear of reprisal what scholarship has discovered—gives vitality to democracy and is the essence of academic freedom. Without these freedoms, academe cannot fulfill its duty to society and may, indeed, become an instrument for the suppression of freedom."

More succinctly but in the same vein, the American Association of University Professors has asserted that "academic freedom has traditionally included the instructor's full freedom as a citizen." (A.A.U.P. Statement on Freedom and Responsibility.)

These formulations of the scope and character of academic freedom are seductively attractive; their appeal to basic constitutional values is difficult to resist. Nonetheless, they reflect a serious error, a mistaken understanding of the true significance of academic freedom. To equate academic freedom with the constitutional freedoms of thought, expression, and assembly which are grounded in the First Amendment is to overlook the fact that the Constitution limits only those actions and decisions for which agencies, institutions, or officers of the State bear a measure of responsibility. This "State action" principle thus precludes the extension of constitutional protection to private institutions of higher education, while it also, to a not insignificant degree, insulates private institutions from sometimes heavy-handed legislative interference.

We may agree enthusiastically with the Supreme Court's ruling in the "flag salute" case:

"If there is any fixed star in our constitutional constellation, it is that no official, high or petty, can prescribe what shall be orthodox in politics, nationalism, religion, or other matters of opinion or force citizens to confess by word or act their faith therein." *(West Virginia Board of Education v. Barnette,* 319 U.S. 624 [1943].)

We may wholeheartedly support the Court's ruling that indiscriminate administrative inquiry into the organizational affiliations of faculty members constitutes a constitutionally impermissible course of action because of its chilling effect upon freedom of thought and assembly. *(Shelton v. Tucker,* 364 U.S. 479 [1960], stating that "the vigilant protection of constitutional freedoms is nowhere more vital than in the community of American schools.") And we may or may not concur with the Court's view that dissemination of a scurrilous and indecent "underground" student newspaper on a university campus cannot properly be made a basis for disciplinary action against the students responsible for the paper because of official objections to the views expressed therein. *(Papish v. University of Missouri,* 410 U.S. 667 [1973].)

But we must remind ourselves that in each of these instances the constitutional impact of the high Court's decisions was limited solely to public educational institutions. Notwithstanding these cases, private colleges and universities remain free, if as a matter of internal polity they so choose, to prescribe the limits of viewpoints and opinions that will be deemed acceptable, the range of faculty organizational memberships which will be tolerated, and the character of publications that will be permitted within the academic environment. Such policy pronouncements by purely private educational authorities would clearly not violate constitutional standards, but in some (although clearly not all) circumstances, could contravene the principles of academic freedom. It seems clear that academic freedom must be recognized as having both a broader application and a narrower focus than the First Amendment.

A second source of ambiguity in the conventional view of academic freedom is the tendency of some misguided faculty members to assume that it embraces every right or freedom claimed to be associated with membership in the college or university community. This wholly erroneous assumption ignores the obvious fact that many justifiable grievances of faculty members are grounded not in the principles of intellectual freedom but in the fundamental liberties which faculty members share with all citizens generally or in similar rights articulated by state laws, institutional policies, regulations, or employment contracts. To blur these sources of faculty protection against arbitrary administrative action weakens academic freedom by trivializing, in many instances, claims to its protection. Almost any effect to enforce a reasonable measure of institutional discipline or to exact compliance with accepted and reasonable standards of academic performance and responsibility tends to elicit a spurious cry that academic freedom is under attack. Even more important, the resulting confusion tends to expose the narrowly

124   VAN ALSTYNE

focused and fundamental principles of academic freedom to the flexible and less reliable standards of judgment that characterize First Amendment litigation.

The Supreme Court has repeatedly affirmed the
rule that First Amendment rights are not absolute but
must be balanced against other interests of society.
For example, the expression of views of a faculty member on matters of public concern ordinarily would not
constitute constitutionally permissible grounds for dismissal of a faculty member of a public college or university, absent a showing of serious disruptive consequences. (See *Pickering v. Board of Education*, 391
U.S. 563 [1968]; *Givhan v. Western Line Consolidated
School Dist.*, 439 U.S. 410 [1979].) But under different circumstances, the balance may be struck against
the claims of free speech. (See *Mount Healthy City
School Dist. v. Doyle*, 429 U.S. 274 [1977].)

In the cited cases, it should be noted, the expressions regarded as objectionable to the employing
authorities were outside the purview of academic freedom. As the 1971 statement of the American Association of State Colleges and Universities rightly pointed
out: "Academic freedom is an additional assurance to
those who teach and pursue knowledge, and, thus,
properly should be restricted to rights of expression
pertaining to teaching and research within their areas
of recognized professional competencies. Beyond this,
expressions by members of the academic community
should carry no more weight or protection than that
accorded any other citizen under the guarantee of
constitutional rights." If the noted distinction is rejected, so that all academic rights are lumped together
under the banners of free speech or of similar pro-

tections of institutional policy in private colleges to which the "State action" limitation precludes constitutional protection, the danger to academic freedom is precisely that it *will* carry "no more weight or protection" than the rights of other citizens. Sound public policy requires that academic freedom be accorded a greater measure of protection than that.

The reasons why academic freedom, properly understood, can claim a special status in the hierarchy of personal rights are linked in part to its unique and indispensable role as the instrument by which the university and society can succeed in their quest for truth, rationality, and responsible critical examination of existing institutions and values. But even more important, academic freedom, by common acceptance, constitutes a great deal more than a mere special privilege enjoyed by scholars. It is also correctly regarded as imposing upon the community of scholars a solemn responsibility to discharge as diligently and effectively as possible the moral responsibilities associated with the university's teaching, research, and public service missions. While all rights imply correlative responsibilities, it is submitted that the obligations of university faculty members may be defined with unusual precision and, unlike the generally more diffused responsibilities associated with other rights, can be enforced by well-established internal institutional procedures such as, although not necessarily limited to, those which characterize the tenure system.

Individual institutional codes, bylaws, regulations, statements, and informal understandings of faculty conduct and responsibilities may differ as to details, but certain primary features are commonly found in all. The strength of academic freedom's claims can be fully assessed only as the moral imperatives underlying these responsibilities become clear.

Responsibility for Academic Integrity

Foremost among these academic responsibilities is a profound commitment to intellectual integrity in the performance of academic work. This commitment embraces both teaching and research. The intentional falsification or distortion of research data or the deliberate misrepresentation of findings and conclusions are clear violations of duty that warrant disciplinary action. The faculty member can be·expected to exercise scrupulous honesty in the communication of opinions and ideas both within and outside the classroom and to demand of himself and others who work under his supervision the maximum of objectivity and accuracy in the search for, analysis, and use of data. To promulgate as received truth those theories or ideas that have not been fully tested and verified by the best and most acceptable intellectual methods and which are therefore still tentative and unsettled would be a grave abuse. To permit the self-interested viewpoints of governmental or corporate sources of funding for academic teaching and research to influence the selection and analysis of data or the conclusions reached would be even worse—a form of intellectual prostitution that is the antithesis of intellectual integrity.

T.R. McConnell has reminded us that "the crises of the moment in our national life are not really in such problems as energy and ecology, complicated and important as they are. Our gravest crises," he notes, "are in confidence, decency, and morality." (T.R. McConnell, in *On the Meaning of the University*, S. McMurrin, Ed., University of Utah Press, 1976, p. 79.) If our universities are to address these basic issues of society, faculty members must demonstrate by both precept and example that integrity in the exercise of intellectual freedom is the cardinal principle of the self-governing society. In Alexander Meikeljohn's words: "Whatever else our students may do or fail to do, they must learn what freedom is. They must learn to believe in it, to love it, and most important of all, to trust it." (A. Meikeljohn, "Professors on Probation," in *Annals of America*, Vol. 16, Encyclopedia Britannica, 1968, p. 604.) In this connection, Walter Lippman perceptively noted that: "The supreme sin of a scholar is to lie, not about where he spent the previous weekend, but about whether two and two make four." (W. Lippman, "The University," in *Annals of America*, Vol. 18, Encyclopedia Britannica, 1968, p. 385.) Only by maintaining an unswerving commitment to the pursuit of truth for its own sake, without regard for external consequences, can the university discharge its goal to serve as a sanctuary for excellence and exemplar of integrity.

Responsibility To Nurture the Moral Dimensions of Human Behavior

As already noted, academic freedom protects the right of the higher education community to discharge its duty to both conserve and reexamine human values in a climate free from external constraints or reprisals.

While a moral consensus on value-related issues may be beyond our reach, a vital component of academic freedom is posited upon the assumption that by asking appropriate questions, seeking objectively for relevant evidence, pursuing the sequential analysis of that evidence, and evaluating alternative consequences of that analysis, rational scholarly activity can provide the bases for judging the morality of human conduct.

It is generally conceded that morality arises from the effort to adjust conflicting or competing claims within the society. But we sometimes overlook the fundamental moral values implicit in academic freedom as the guardian of a participatory process by which the most basic ideas can be sifted, analyzed, tested, and weighed in the search for an acceptable balance between conflicting social, economic, and political pressures. The fundamental premises of academic freedom are that truth has always had moral value and that man's obligation and virtue is to find it and live in accordance with it.

While we properly yearn to be free from the constraints imposed by the unsavory excesses of the past—e.g., religious intolerance, slavery, the robber barons, social and economic discrimination against minorities, child labor, slumlords, etc.—we should not shirk the task of extracting and preserving enduring values from the tangled skeins of human experience. As Frederic W. Maitland once wisely observed, "Today we study the day before yesterday in order that yesterday may not paralyze today, and today may not paralyze tomorow." In short, while academic freedom is properly concerned with what is or has been, it must also be concerned with what ought to be.

In his *Outline of History,* H.G. Wells suggested that "human history becomes more and more a race between education and catastrophe." We face the reality of this dictum as we contemplate the fact that humankind has the capacity to maintain great societies or stage unthinkable holocausts, to ennoble life or disfigure it, to nurture the human condition or utterly destroy civilization. It follows that one of the most pressing moral imperatives of education is to lay a basic foundation of those liberal values which link ourselves with the mainstream of humanity. We must not forget that knowledge without integrity is dangerous and that knowledge without justice is mere cunning.

Higher education, when properly committed to the development of basic moral sensitivities, has the capacity to strengthen and revitalize our cultural heritage by insisting that human attitudes and conduct should be rooted in the highest values of self and society. By precept and example, the university can demonstrate that in the rational processes associated with freedom of the mind lies the salvation of humankind. The intellectual liberation that emerges from morally focused higher education, in Howard R. Bowen's words, "implies freedom from prejudice, openness to new ideas, acceptance of change, and tolerance of persons of differing ideologies, cultures, and races. It is favorable to historical and geographical perspective, appreciation of different cultures, a cosmopolitan outlook, and international understanding. It encourages individuality—as distinct from conformity—among persons. It leads to wide and rapid diffusion of new ideas and new technologies.

And it is conducive to social change." (H.R. Bowen, *The State of the Nation and the Agenda for Higher Education*, Jossey-Bass, 1982, p. 121.)

To be worthy of its finest potential, the higher education community has a profound obligation to celebrate the values implicit in human freedom that radiate from our common cultural heritage.

In his 1984 Jefferson Lecture, Dr. Sidney Hook has noted the disquieting symptoms of an eroding allegiance to the ideals of the self-governing society in the United States, an erosion which he describes as an "urgent contemporary crisis." Among these phenomena, he lists "(1) the vehement assertion of rights and entitlements without the acceptance of corresponding duties and obligations; (2) the invocation of group rights to justify overriding the rights of individuals; (3) the growth of violence, and the toleration of violence in schools and local assemblies; (4) the open defiance of laws authorized by democratic process, and the indulgence of courts toward repeated and unrepentant violators; (5) the continued invasion by the courts themselves into the legislative process; (6) the loss of faith in the electorate as the ultimate custodian of its own freedom." (Hook, "Education in Defense of a Free Society," *Commentary*, July 1984, p. 17 at 21.) Faced with these threats to the democratic ethos from within, Dr. Hook questions whether we continue to possess the necessary social solidarity and cohesion to meet the challenges to the self-governing society which come from without, particularly the threat posed by the global expansion of Communism. As a remedy, consistent with the Jeffersonian faith in an educated citizenry, he appeals for greater emphasis on educational programs designed to sharpen students' understanding of the free society, its history and heroes, its achievements and failures, its challenges and dangers, in contrast to the closed totalitarian world.

Humankind has unique capacities to love and to dream, extend compassion and understanding to others, govern itself freely and democratically, experience inspiration, formulate and pursue goals, exercise imagination, think in abstract terms, feel the power of conscience, cope with imponderables, and sense the universal brotherhood of man. These qualities, once awakened, insistently call upon the educated individual to assume a measure of responsibility for his fellow human beings and to transmit to future generations the cultural heritage and its moral values not only unimpaired but improved wherever possible. They are a subtle reminder that no person can be truly at peace with himself if he does not live up to his moral capacity.

A fully educated individual is one who has learned to avoid the common hazards to clear thinking—hazards such as provincialism, irrational prejudice, self-interest, intolerance of uncertainty and ambiguity, over-dependence on familiar categories of thought, and excessive sentimentality. He or she is emancipated from prejudice and dogma, has reasonable understanding of his or her environment, is able to weigh evidence and form independent judgments about ideas and idealogies, is capable of making wise choices that may affect his or her personal well-being and that of mankind generally, and can anticipate and provide for connections between causes and effects.

He appreciates the significance of analogies, is sensitive to the dangers of unquestioned adherence to precedent, and is not intimidated by intellectual complexity. But notwithstanding all of these and other unique potential characteristics of human beings which higher education may cultivate and cause to blossom, it remains true that education not grounded upon solid moral foundations and a sense of social responsibility would be no better than ignorance. Our belief in education is, in the long run, based upon the faith that the maximum development of the human potential will produce individual and social benefits of incalculable value. It is thus one of the levers by which humankind can control its own destiny.

As Terance Sandalow had reminded us, one of the grand goals of education is to develop character—the aggregate of those personal qualities which are necessary to steadfastness of purpose in the face of the disappointments, fears, pains, temptations, and other obstacles which are the common experience of mankind. "Courage, patience, perseverance, and other qualities that enable us to overcome these impediments," he observes, "are, for that reason, universally regarded as virtues, and since they are necessary to the success of any sustained moral undertaking, they have a special claim to our attention [as educators]." (Sandalow, "The Moral Responsibility of Law Schools," *Journal of Legal Education*, June 1984.)

To quote Howard Bowen once more: "We can be certain that education will not bring heaven on earth. It will not obliterate all aggression, selfishness, conflict, sloth, or effeteness. But it could help make life more humane and more abundant or at least help to keep it from becoming grossly uncivilized." *(Ibid.,* p. 124.) These results, however, are likely to flow most abundantly from education that seeks intentionally to build character upon the basis of moral principles, celebrates the code of service to one's fellowmen, constantly reaffirms the rule of law based on due process and equality of opportunity as the basis of the free society, and firmly articulates the need for a compassionate understanding of the bonds of human brotherhood. (See A. Cecil, *The Foundations of a Free Society,* 1983, *passim.)*

Responsibility for Competence in the Quest for Truth

As we have already noted, academic freedom provides the essential environment in which the continuing search for truth may proceed. It does not, however, provide assurance that new knowledge, insights, opinions, or ideas that emerge in the quest for truth are, in fact, true. Only intellectual arrogance or ideological conviction would assert the contrary.

The free self-governing society posits its moral strength on the proposition that laws and the institutions of public order associated with the implementation of laws are fundamentally justified because they reflect a continuing faith in and commitment to the achievement of freedom and justice based on the substantial foundation of truth as we now understand it. On the other hand, the transcendent values which we ascribe to freedom of thought and its inescapable corollary of the right of dissent as the keystones of the self-governing society compel accep-

tance of the principle that received knowledge, even
though parading in the garb of truth, is always subject
to reexamination. The responsible scholar proceeds
with the task of scholarship in spite of, and indeed
because of, a healthy realization that received premises may be flawed or data deficient, the understanding that the truths of yesterday have often been found
to be insupportable in modern context, and a recognition that claims to absolute truth may all too easily
become oppressive dogma. As Justice Oliver Wendell
Holmes, Jr., pointed out: " . . . when men have realized that time has upset many fighting faiths, they may
come to believe even more than they believe the very
foundations of their own conduct that the ultimate
good desired is better reached by free trade in ideas—
that the best test of truth is the power of the thought to
get itself accepted in the competition of the market,
and that truth is the only ground upon which their
wishes can be safely carried out." (*Abrams v. United
States*, 250 U.S. 616 [1919], dissenting opinion.)

As Professor Samuel Enoch Stumpf has cogently
argued, the democratic conception of truth holds that
"while there may be an absolute truth, no one has it
absolutely."

This is not to say that there are no absolute truths;
obviously, factual propositions must be either true or
false. But it does imply, correctly I believe, that we
cannot know with certainty whether a particular factual proposition is absolutely true or absolutely false.

The society of free men and women, therefore,
must insist on the right of dissent, since it is committed to the paradoxical view that truth can be found
but no existing expression of truth can be regarded

with certainty and as beyond challenge. The search for truth is basically a search for reality, an effort to dispel illusion. In Professor Stumpf's words: "The conviction that there is some ground for truth, that the human mind has the capacity to approximate it, and that the minds of most men [and women] under conditions of free inquiry will achieve workable degrees of agreement on it is what provides an open society with the willingness and courage to assume the risk of the free flow of ideas. The conviction that all formulations of truth are in some sense relative is what provides men in a free society with the sense of urgency to pursue the truth to new heights." (Samuel E. Stumpf, "Freedom to Learn," in *Free Man vs. His Government*, A.L. Hardin, Ed., Southern Methodist University Press, 1958, pp. 51-52.)

An indispensable corollary of academic freedom, therefore, is the responsibility of the academic scholar to strive constantly to achieve and maintain the highest possible level of professional competence in the field of his or her expertise, coupled with an informed awareness, so far as reasonably available, of work being done in that field by other competent scholars, so that the search for truth may proceed at its cutting edge, unabated by lethargy, inertia, or complacency.

On a possibly less fundamental but not less important level, the faculty member's obligation to develop and maintain competence also extends to the honing of communicative and teaching skills, the sharpening of abilities to use available instructional equipment effectively, and the fulfillment of academic obligations to discharge academic assignments, meet scheduled classes punctually, arrange for student conferences for counsel and advice, and participate in essential collegial tasks such as the filing of required reports and attendance at established committee meetings. It has been repeatedly affirmed in the courts that incompetence or intransigence in these respects are permissible grounds for dismissal of tenured faculty members and do not violate the principles of academic freedom. (See *Smith v. Kent State University*, 696 F.2d 476 [6th Cir. 1983]; *Chung v. Park*, 377 F. Supp. 524 [D. Md. 1974]; *Jawa v. Fayetteville State University*, 426 F. Supp. 218 [D.N.C. 1976]; *Saunders v. Reorganized School Dist. No. 2 of Osage County*, 520 S.W.2d 29 [Mo. 1975].)

Responsibility To Establish and Protect an Effective Learning Environment

A fourth responsibility implicit in the obligations of academic freedom involves a commitment by members of the academic community to establish and protect a campus environment conducive to effective learning and the orderly discharge of academic functions. Open and rational discussion in an atmosphere of mutual respect is the primary means implied by the obligations of academic freedom for the clarification and resolution of debatable issues. Participation in, or the encouragement of, violence, harassment, intimidation, extreme vulgarity, ribald behavior, and other forms of disruption of orderly academic affairs should be recognized as serious and indefensible breaches of this obligation to maintain civility of discourse.

Recent court decisions have properly concluded

that faculty members who persistently ignore appropriate standards of institutional dignity, decorum, and
mutual respect, demonstrating a lack of appropriate
candor, restraint, and sensitivity in the classroom or in
interfaculty relationships, may under some circumstances justifiably be denied tenure (see *Mayberry v.
Dies*, 663 F.2d 502 [4th Cir. 1981], cert. denied, 459
U.S. 830 [1982]), or be visited with disciplinary sanctions despite tenured status. (See *Landrum v. Eastern
Kentucky University*, 578 F. Supp. 241 [D. Ky. Jan.
16, 1984]; *Palo Verde Unified School Dist. v. Hensey*,
4 Cal. App. 3d 967, 88 Cal. Rptr. 570 [1970].) Similarly, faculty members cannot claim protection on
grounds of academic freedom for condoning or engaging in sexual harassment of female students. (See *Ross
v. Robb*, 662 S.W.2d 257 [Mo. 1983]; *Lehman v.
Board of Trustees of Whitman College*, 89 Wash. 2d
874, 576 P.2d 392 [1978].) Nor can they make such
claims for engaging in offensive homosexual advances
to male students. (See *Korf v. Ball State University*,
726 F.2d 1222 [7th Cir. 1984].) Moreover, serious
violations of the law or evidence of conduct involving
moral turpitude in off-campus activities may also pol-
lute the academic atmosphere to a degree sufficient to
warrant suspension or expulsion from the community
of scholars. (See *Perryman v. School Committee of
Boston*, 458 N.E.2d 748 [Mass. App. 1983] [welfare
fraud]; *Board of Trustees v. Stubblefield*, 16 Cal. App.
3d 820, 94 Cal. Rptr. 318 [1971] [public nudity and
assault on a police officer].)

A vital manifestation of the effective learning environment that is of special concern relates to the
classroom atmosphere. College and university faculty

members should never yield to the temptation to use their domination of the classroom as a setting for indoctrination of students into particular ideologies, theories, or convictions. Efforts to secure assent to beliefs by nonrational means are characteristic of education in totalitarian regimes but are anathema to the concept of academic freedom.

As one court has observed, a university has the responsibility "to maintain a competition of different views in the classroom and to prevent the use of the classroom by a teacher deliberately to proselytize for a certain cause or knowingly to emphasize only that selection of data best enforcing to his own personal biases." (*Keddie v. Pennsylvania State University,* 412 F. Supp. 1264 [D. Pa. 1976].) The critical, reflective, and questioning spirit that underpins our free society should prevail constantly in all aspects of classroom teaching.

The effective learning environment, however, extends well beyond the obvious need for civility of discourse in an atmosphere of shared intellectual respect. It requires arrangements calculated to enhance the optimal personal involvement of students and faculty members in the educational process through flexible interaction at several discrete levels. It also demands unremitting attention to the striking of an acceptable balance between competing curricular demands, the development of academic policies which do not yield too easily to narrowly defined vocationalism or to immediate utilitarian objectives at the expense of more broadly conceived liberal and humanitarian impulses. This is not to suggest that vocational education cannot be truly effective in the absence of important components of liberal studies; it does, however, recognize that an appreciation for the primary roots of our moral heritage is nurtured and tends to flourish best in the context of a liberal and humanitarian educational core.

Finally, the effective learning environment must seek by all reasonable means to prevent the locking up of basic research findings and conclusions through artificial constraints upon the flow of information, technical data, and scientific ideas. While recent efforts on the part of government contracting and granting agencies to classify such material in restrictive ways stress the national security implications of unlimited disclosure, they fail to give adequate weight in many instances to the facts that human knowledge does not stay put and that the sharing of such knowledge is essential to intellectual progress in all fields of human activity.

Responsibility for Effective Functioning of the Tenure System

As noted above, the primary protection of academic freedom on most campuses resides in the system of academic tenure. While the judicial system may serve as an ultimate, although cumbersome and limited, safeguard in certain cases, the tenured faculty members of the institution bear the responsibility to organize, administer, and assure the integrity of the internal review and appeal procedures by which allegations of abridgement of academic freedom by tenured and nontenured faculty alike are investigated and resolved. Except where limited by commonly accepted institutional standards (e.g., the policies of private denominational institutions against heresy), academic freedom is the right and duty of all members of the college or university community. But only the tenured faculty generally enjoy the clear legal protection and institutional authority necessary to an independent, vigorous, and fearless exposure and condemnation of improper influences seeking to undermine the structure of academic freedom. The legal status of a tenured faculty member is widely recognized to be that of the holder of a vested property interest secured by constitutional or contractual principles enforceable in law *(Perry v. Sinderman, supra)*. The nontenured member, however, enjoys no such protection and could be readily dismissed or disciplined by an administrator insensitive to the demands of academic freedom, were it not for the protective authority of the tenured faculty and its authorized governance arrangements. Indeed, the very existence of internal academic procedures and their related peer group committee structures administered by the tenured faculty constitute such a major source of assurance that challenges to academic freedom are infrequently mounted.

It follows that a major moral obligation of the faculty and administration is to demand assurances that wherever a tenure system obtains, it is functioning with integrity and effectiveness. Recruitment of tenure-track faculty must be based on rigorous academic qualifications consistent with principles of equal opportunity. Competence reviews during the pretenure probationary period must be thorough and searching. The ultimate award of tenure must be limited to those members of the profession who not only exemplify the highest standards of teaching excellence and scholarship but also demonstrate a commitment to the purposes and responsibilities inherent in the principle of academic freedom. Posttenure review of faculty competence and performance not only should be routinely provided but must also be thorough and fair; routine and perfunctory procedures that water down the meaning of "good cause" for academic termination are a disservice to the profession, tend to undermine public support for the tenure system, and are prejudicial to the preservation of academic freedom. Tenure was never intended to be, and must not be allowed to become, a haven for imcompetence or irresponsibility. To the extent that faculties in some institutions concededly have emphasized tenure as a symbol of job security rather than as a bulwark for academic freedom, the latter interest has and will continue inevitably to erode.

The several responsibilities associated with academic freedom that are sketched above do not necessarily exhaust the topic. They do, however, illustrate the thesis that academic freedom should be regarded primarily as a moral duty and not as a privilege. Properly implemented, it provides the impetus for an educational experience that conveys to the student an appreciation for what it means to be a free individual, an understanding of the issues of life which successive ages of mankind have faced, and a sensitivity to the reality behind those elements of personal character which we describe as loyalty, commitment, conscience, and integrity.

As Sterling McMurrin has cogently argued, the primary contribution of educational institutions to the moral strength of society lies in the cultivation of reasoning capacity, "the reason that can grasp the universal in the particular, assess the quality of arguments, analyze the worth of competing values, expose prejudice, temper the emotions, and provide the ground for intelligent decision and action." (S. McMurrin, "Education and Moral Values," in *Conflict and Harmony, Andrew R. Cecil Lectures on Moral Values in a Free Society,* Vol. 3, 1982, p. 211.) A continuing commitment by educators to the strengthening of such reasoning capacity can exert a powerful influence upon the revitalization of individual moral responsibility as the cornerstone of our polity. A broadly based commitment to the life of reason, nurtured in the atmosphere of academic freedom, promises to oppose the increasing irrationality and hedonism of society, the tendency to identify narrow self-interest rather than the general welfare as the keystone of policy, the growing trivialization and demagoguery of political campaign tactics, the excessive bureaucratization of governmental and private organizations, and the continued depersonalization of human relationships by a burgeoning technology.

The moral responsibilities associated with academic freedom thus call to mind the image of the ideal university, in the evocative words of Rabindinrath Tagore, as a place

" . . . where tireless striving stretches its
arms toward perfection,
Where the clear stream of reason
has not lost its way into the
dreary sand of dead habit;
Where the mind is led forward . . .
into ever-widening thought and
action."

ECONOMIC FREEDOM:
THE RIGHTS AND RESPONSIBILITIES OF THE ENTREPRENEUR IN OUR MIXED ECONOMY

by

Andrew R. Cecil

Andrew R. Cecil

Dr. Cecil is Distinguished Scholar in Residence at The University of Texas at Dallas and Chancellor Emeritus and Trustee of The Southwestern Legal Foundation.

Associated with the Foundation since 1958, Dr. Cecil helped guide its development of five educational centers that offer nationally and internationally recognized programs in advanced continuing education.

In February 1979 the University established in his honor the Andrew R. Cecil Lectures on Moral Values in a Free Society, and invited Dr. Cecil to deliver the first series of lectures in November 1979. The first annual proceedings were published as Dr. Cecil's book The Third Way: Enlightened Capitalism and the Search for a New Social Order, *which received an enthusiastic response. He also lectured in each subsequent series. A new book,* The Foundations of a Free Society, *was published in 1983.*

Educated in Europe and well launched on a career as a professor and practitioner in the fields of law and economics, Dr. Cecil resumed his academic career after World War II in Lima, Peru, at the University of San Marcos. After 1949, he was associated with the Methodist church-affiliated colleges and universities in the United States until he joined the Foundation. He is author of twelve books on the subjects of law and economics and of more than seventy articles on these subjects and on the philosophy of religion published in periodicals and anthologies.

A member of the American Society of International Law, of the American Branch of the International Law Association, and of the American Judicature Society, Dr. Cecil has served on numerous commissions for the Methodist Church, and is a member of the Board of Trustees of the National Methodist Foundation for Christian Higher Education. In 1981 he was named an Honorary Rotarian.

ECONOMIC FREEDOM:
THE RIGHTS AND RESPONSIBILITIES OF THE ENTREPRENEUR IN OUR MIXED ECONOMY

by

Andrew R. Cecil

"In the first place, the American people are good; their mentality is settled and pervasive; they are devoted and ingenious in improving the instruments of material economy: and it is precisely in this sphere that they would have been called upon to act for the welfare of all mankind."
—George Santayana, *Dominations and Powers*

Economic Liberalism

Modern capitalism and the business entrepreneur appeared in the eighteenth century as British inventions. The Industrial Revolution—which started in Great Britain about the year 1750, spread to the Continent, and foreshadowed a millenium for economic liberalism—stemmed doctrinally in the eighteenth century from the French Physiocrats and the Scottish economist Adam Smith, whose great work, commonly called "The Wealth of Nations," has won him recognition as "the father of political economy." The commercial rivalry for markets called for freedom of trade and freedom of contract with a minimum of restric-

147

tions by State, church, or labor organizations on economic self-interest and on the desire for economic or pecuniary gain. A system of prices freely determined in the market by the interaction of the law of supply and demand became the fundamental characteristic of the capitalistic economy.

In 1859 Darwin published *The Origin of Species by Means of Natural Selection, or the Preservation of Favored Races in the Struggle for Life*, which revealed his hypothesis of the evolutionary conception of the universe. The evolutionary doctrine proclaimed, in Darwin's own words, that

> "As many more individuals of each species are born than can possibly survive, and as, consequently, there is a frequently recurring struggle for existence, it follows that any being, if it vary however slightly in any manner profitable to itself, under the complex and sometimes varying conditions of life, will have a better chance of surviving, and thus be *naturally selected*. From the strong principle of inheritance, any selected variety will tend to propagate its new and modified form."

The Darwinist doctrines of "the survival of the fittest" and "the persistence of force" were extended from the realm of natural science to those of the history of mankind (to explain the struggle between nations, races, and classes), anthropology, psychology, ethics, and sociology. When applied to international affairs, they implied the right of the "big powers" to govern and the destiny of the "lesser powers" to be governed. The Darwinist doctrine of a "struggle for existence," when applied to economic life, led into a stage of economic liberalism which encouraged free competition, individual initiative unhampered by governmental interference and regulations, and large-scale capitalistic enterprise. The growth of capitalism, conjoined with the development of modern science and the rise of nationalism, was marked by an expansion of trade and a new economic imperialism turned to the task of colonizing the world. Fierce social convulsion was caused by a swift increase in the wealth of new classes and by a deepened depression of the old, poor, and exploited classes.

Martin Luther's denunciations of exploitation and of the concentration of power that resulted from the economic revolution of the sixteenth century were applicable to the Industrial Revolution that took place three centuries later. The prophetic genius of the Reformation wrote in *The Large Catechism,* in explaining the meaning of the Seventh Commandment, "Thou shalt not steal":

> "These are also men whom you may call gentlemen—robbers, land grabbers, and road agents, quite above the safe-robber or pilferer of petty cash. These occupy seats of honor, are styled great lords and honorable, pious citizens, and under the cloak of honesty they rob and steal. Yea, we might well let the lesser individual thieves alone if we could only arrest the great, powerful arch-thieves."

In the name of freedom of contract and personal liberty, economic liberalism opposed labor organizations and labor legislation, leaving the workers at the employers' mercy. The "wage slavery" formulated by David Ricardo in his subsistence theory provided that "the natural price of labor is that which is necessary to enable laborers, one with another, to subsist and to perpetuate their race, without either increase or diminution." Labor was regarded as a commodity, and wages, like other commodities, were left to the free competition of the market with no interference by the State, guilds, trade unions, or the church. Wages, like the price of commodities, were determined by the law of supply and demand.

Reaction to Laissez-Faire Liberalism

It is not surprising that the excesses of such a heartless capitalism brought a passionate anticapitalist reaction. The Luddites, workmen of the industrial centers of England in 1812-1818 (named for Ned Ludd, a semilegendary figure who was said to have destroyed stocking frames in a revolt against their owners), systematically wrecked machinery, to which they attributed the displacement caused by technological changes and the prevailing unemployment and misery of working people. The exploitation, industrial strife, and social evils caused by heartless capitalism were depicted by writers who acted as a kind of conscience for Western society. Charles Dickens (1812-1870) drew attention to the practice of child labor and other abuses of children in novels such as *Hard Times, Oliver Twist*, and *Nicholas Nickleby*, illustrating the child as a victim of social evils of his day.

In Germany, the most significant drama of Gerhart Hauptmann (1862-1946), one of the leading figures of modern German literature, was the famous play *The Weavers*, which won him worldwide recognition. When the play was produced in Berlin and Paris, it received some of the most enthusiastic demonstrations ever accorded a play. The drama deals with a collective group of some seventy characters. It descends to the depths of the workers' misfortunes, and it depicts the circumstances surrounding a historical uprising of a group of textile workers that had occurred in the Eulengebirge region of Germany in the 1840s. Desperate and hungry, the workers wreck their employer's home and destroy the machines upon which they blame their misery. The suffering and the meager lives of the workers are shown to be the direct fault of the economic system in which they toil. (Hauptmann, who received the Nobel Prize in 1912, espoused a number of literary movements; his plays after 1912—in the last twenty-five years of his life—were of no particular importance, and his fame was tarnished by his association with the Hitler regime.)

In the United States the novelist Upton Sinclair (1878-1968) became an inspiration for social change because of his treatment of the social evils caused by unrestricted corporate activity. His novel *The Jungle* (1905) exposed conditions in Chicago stockyards and led to an investigation which was followed by improvements in those conditions.

The poor, the socially and economically weak, and the exploited became the primary concern of the church. In 1891 Pope Leo XIII issued his far-reaching

encyclical *Rerum novarum.* Addressed primarily to
European countries, it raised a powerful voice of op-
position against the shameful treatment of men "like
chattels to make money by" and against "the
wretchedness pressing so heavily and unjustly at this
moment on the vast majority of working classes." The
encyclical emphasized that "labor is not a commodity"
and sought remedies against the very rich men who
"have been able to lay upon the teeming masses of the
laboring poor a yoke little better than that of slavery
itself."

Among the suggested remedies were legislation to
"protect women and children from oppressive employment" and help from the State for wage earners,
"who are undoubtedly among the weak and
necessitous" and, therefore, "should be specially
cared for and protected by the commonwealth." Thus,
the Pope challenged the philosophy of laissez-faire
which advocated for the State the role of a "passive
policeman" with functions limited to the preservation
of public order and protection of private property.

The problems caused by the mechanization and industrialization that followed the Civil War and the
mass immigration from abroad prompted the church
in the United States to turn to social problems caused
by industrialization and laissez-faire practice. The
message of the "Social Gospel" called for public justice
and a righteousness that would eliminate the corruption of the powerful and the poverty of the helpless
and weak. The Social Gospel, opposed in its beginning
by conservative Protestantism as a program of humanitarian reform rather than an expression of Christian

faith, found a dynamic exponent in a professor at the Rochester Theological Seminary, Walter Rauschenbush.

The doctrine of the Kingdom of God, according to Rauschenbush, is itself the Social Gospel and it embraces all of human life. The church, he wrote, "is one social institution alongside of the family, the industrial organization, and the State . . . The Church is indispensable to the religious education of humanity and to the conservation of religion, but the greatest future awaits religion in the public life of humanity." Rauschenbush did not question the effectiveness of the capitalistic method of the production of wealth evidence by modern civilization. He was appalled, however, by the "capitalistic methods in the production of human wreckage." In his *A Theology for the Social Gospel,* he stressed that

> "one-sided control of economic power tempts to exploitation and oppression; it directs the productive process of society primarily toward the creation of private profit rather than the service of human needs; it demands autocratic management and strengthens the autocratic principle in all social affairs; it has impressed a materialistic spirit on our whole civilization."

The fundamental step of repentance and conversion for professions and organizatons is, according to Rauschenbush, "to give up monopoly power and the incomes derived from legalized extortion, and to come under the law of service, content with a fair income for honest work."

The doctrine of rigidly limited functions of the State is historically not conservatism but rather nineteenth-century laissez-faire liberalism. (Ironically, certain aspects of the nineteenth-century liberalism became the creed of the twentieth-century conservatism.) Only when some liberals began to realize that among the effects of unrestrained industrial capitalism was the destruction of men's spirits and personalities did they embark on the venture of seeking a new order of justice.

The liberals who abandoned nineteenth-century liberalism sought an order of integrity for the political and economic life of society that would free it from the darkness of corruption and degeneration that emerged under the practice of economic liberalism. The restrictive *ad hoc* measures against a self-regulating market such as the English Health and Morals Act of 1802 relating to child labor, the act that further restricted employment of children (1819), the granting of the right to form labor unions (1824), or the liberalization of poor laws (1834) did not remove, however, the difficulties encountered under the system of laissez-faire. The human predicaments and social disorder caused by the Industrial Revolution were the potent forces that led toward communism, one of the greatest tragedies in the history of mankind and one that has no precedent in its inhumanity.

Oppression Under Communism

All the violent revolutions of this century have demonstrated that when a revolution falls into the hands of fanatical tyrants they repress more people than the government they replaced. This is also true of the communist revolution that created the Soviet Union. Instead of emancipating the masses as it promised, the new ruling class—the communist party—sacrificed them to achieve an unrestrained power that seems never to satisfy the communist dictators.

In order to cling to power, the rulers of Soviet Russia plunged their country into massive famines. With contemptuous disregard for the everyday basic needs of the population, they depopulated towns and regions; destroyed the nation's agricultural economy, annihilating millions of peasants for the sake of the concept of the collective farm; and filled prisons and concentration camps with industrial workers who were sacrificed as scapegoats for not achieving the unattainable goals of the planned economy and its periodically proclaimed five-year plans.

After nearly seventy years of experimentation, the communist countries cannot feed or house their people adequately. In Soviet Russia the imports of food increase each year. The two percent of the land which the State allows to farmers for private cultivation generates one-third of the total production of meat, eggs, milk, and vegetables.

The government has complete control of industry, and management and the workers are under constant threat of prosecution. This can be illustrated by a true story. During World War II, a bakery had to deliver bread to the army, but there were no trucks. The brick kiln, which was in the neighborhood, had trucks, but the drivers asked for bread in payment for making

deliveries for the bakery. The manager of the bakery
thus faced a serious problem. If he failed to deliver the
bread, he could be sent to prison for sabotage of the
war effort; on the other hand, if he gave bread to the
drivers, he could be sentenced for "squandering" the
government's property. Finally, after an agonizing
procrastination, the manager decided to use the drivers and to transfer the bread at night. He released the
night watchman so as to eliminate any witness to his
"crime." Watching by the door, he handed each driver
a loaf of bread. This precaution, however, did not help
him to escape punishment since he was denounced by
his assistant.

What means of resistance are left to such an oppressed population? Alexander Solzhenitsyn writes:

> "From ancient times theft was looked upon as a
> deadly sin in Russia, but today stealing from the
> government has become a common, universally
> understood fact of life, an act necessary for sur-
> vival. Through theft the people recover part of
> their rights, and this form of self-defense causes
> tremendous harm to the government. . . . No one
> has any desire to work honestly for the benefit of a
> dishonest regime." ("Communism at the End of
> the Brezhnev Regime," *National Review*, January
> 21, 1983, p. 33.)

In a responsible society, in which moral and spiritual values play an important role, the concept of
business enterprise transcends both the evil alterna-
tives which have just been described. Such a society

avoids both the cruel power of unhampered industrial capitalism of the 1800s and the darkness of tyranny, corruption, and poverty offered by present communism. What kind of business enterprise, then, can we expect in a free society where righteousness guides men and their domestic, economic, and political institutions?

Wealth

To answer this question we must first throw light upon the dilemma: Is wealth a source of evil? (By wealth, we mean material riches rather than the economic concept of wealth defined as the stock of economic goods in existence.) Is profit a respectable economic factor rather than a dirty word implying harm done to one's neighbor, taking advantage of him in a business transaction?

Private ownership in itself is not an issue. The right to own personal property is recognized by the very existence of the Commandment "Thou shalt not steal," a Commandment vigorously reinforced by the prophets, who condemned offenses against this Commandment. Jesus thought of material and not spiritual needs when he prayed, "Give us this day our daily bread." But he was very forthright about the spiritual dangers and temptations of wealth.

As early as in the beginning of the third century, Clement of Alexandria—commenting in his "The Rich Man's Salvation" on the biblical story of the rich young man who wanted to be sure of eternal life— distinguished inner detachment from wealth from outer renunciation of wealth regardless of its use. Clement of Alexandria was among the first Christian thinkers who tried to bring together a Christian, compassionate concern for one's neighbor with a Greek philosophy marked by individualism and the pursuit of the good life.

Referring to Jesus's warning about the danger of riches—"It is easier for a camel to go through the eye of a needle than for a rich man to enter the kingdom of God" (Mark 10:25), Clement asked whether the "beggars for their daily bread, the poor dispersed on the streets, who know not God and God's righteousness, simply on account of their extreme want and destitution of subsistence, and lack even of the smallest things, were most blessed and most dear to God, and sole posessors of everlasting life?"

Not at all, Clement maintained. Such an interpretation would be irrational. Without wealth, how could we feed the hungry, provide shelter to the homeless, and clothe the naked? Riches are a gift of God provided for the use and benefit of our neighbor. Referring to the advice Jesus gave the rich young man— "Go, sell what you have, and give to the poor, and you will have treasure in heaven" (Mark 10:21), Clement rejected the idea that wealth should be cast away, for the disposition of it is no advantage to the one who has deprived himself of what is serviceable, nor to the needy and the poor. "The renunciation, then, and selling of all possessions, is to be understood as spoken of the passions of the soul."

What are these passions of the soul of which Clement writes? He cites both the excitement and morbid feelings of greed and the anxieties of want that are the thorns of existence and choke the seed of life. Those who take advantage of wealth to destroy others are condemned, but those who learn to use their wealth for the benefit of all may use it to buy eternal life. Riches can be a blessing or a curse, depending on the mental disposition and on the actions of the one possessing them. The ideal is to be superior to the possession of wealth, not the slave of the things one possesses. This spiritual detachment enables wealth to be a positive benefit to everyone in the community.

The issues of wealth, of commerical practice, and of finding just solutions to economic and social problems continued to be of great concern to founders of the Reformation and to the theologians and church leaders who succeeded them. During the economic revolution that accompanied the Renaissance, Martin Luther, who hated capitalism and monopolies and distrusted merchants (and also peasants), denounced the payment of interest and the concessions made by the church. He wrote: "The greatest misfortune of the German nation is easily the traffic in interest . . . The devil invented it, and the Pope by giving his sanction to it, has done untold evil throughout the world."

Calvin took a position on interest payments more appealing to the business world. He accepted the realities of commercial practice and urged his followers to solve problems of economic and social problems in the light of existing circumstances. On the subject of usury, he argued that because of changed conditions Christians should not be guided by the Holy Scripture but by dictates of natural justice and the Golden Rule.

During the early history of the Hebrews, they led an
agricultural and pastoral life, and the loans were made
not as capital investments in a business but rather to
help someone out of debt. (The law of Moses forbade a
Hebrew from taking interest on money he loaned to a
brother Hebrew as a matter of charity.) Payment of
interest for capital is as reasonable, Calvin maintained,
as the payment of rent; because capital and credit are
indispensable, the payment of interest is in accord
with commercial common sense, and only extortion is
to be avoided. The Larger Catechism of the
Westminster Confession—the most celebrated pronouncement of English-speaking Calvinism—referred
in Question 141 to the Eighth Commandment ("Thou
shalt not steal") and listed among the duties the Commandment entails "an endeavor by all just and lawful
means to procure, preserve, and further the wealth
and outward estate of others, as well as our own."
R. H. Tawney, the English economist, wrote in his
Religion and the Rise of Capitalism: "Calvin did for
the *bourgeoisie* of the sixteenth century what Marx did
for the proletariat of the nineteenth."

John Wesley (1703-1791), the father of the Methodist renewal, also saw the need for solving economic
problems in the light of changing conditions. He
asserted that "in the present state of mankind, wealth
is an excellent gift of God, answering the noblest
ends." The important thing to Wesley was that men
learn how to employ wealth to these "noblest ends."
These ends include food and drink for the hungry and
thirsty, clothing for the naked, shelter for the homeless, and care for the widow, the orphan, the sick, and

the oppressed. The love of money, not money itself, is the "root of all evil." It may be used for ill or may be used for the best service in all the affairs of life; it may be, states Wesley, "as eyes to the blind, as feet to the lame; yea, a lifter up from the gates of death."

Jesus' advice—"I say unto you, make to yourselves friends of the mammon of unrighteousness; that, when ye fail, they may receive you into everlasting habitations" (Luke 16:9)—is the subject of Wesley's sermon "On the Use of Money." To become faithful stewards of the "mammon of unrighteousness," Wesley suggests following three rules: "Gain all you can"; "Save all you can"; and "Give all you can."

Wesley regarded it as man's bounden duty to acquire wealth without hurting his body, his mind, or his neighbor. Our business activities cannot be destructive to our health or strength; they must be consistent with a good conscience and with brotherly love. We cannot, therefore, "sell our goods below the market price; we cannot study to ruin our neighbor's trade, in order to advance our own. . . . None can gain by swallowing up his neighbor's substance without gaining the damnation of hell!"

Having gained all we can by using honest wisdom and the understanding which God has given us, we have to follow the second rule of Christian prudence by saving all we can. God placed us on the earth not as proprietors but as stewards, in whose hands the Lord's goods have been lodged, "but with the right of resuming whenever it pleases Him." The sole property of these goods, states Wesley, "rests in Him, nor can ever be alienated from Him." By saving we can provide things needful for ourselves and our family and "do good to them that are of the household of faith" and, when overflow is left, "do good to all men."

Reconciling Wealth and Profits
With Economic Ethics

The question of reconciling wealth and profits with Christ's discipleship has been a matter of continued debate among theologians and philosophers. The point of view of Clement of Alexandria, outlined above, would not appeal to those who favored the monastic discipline, which calls for renunciation of the world's standards of value and of worldly possessions. But it did appeal to the prosperous Christians in Alexandria, just as it appeals to American society today.

Calvin and Luther believed in the dignity and equality of all kinds of work. They also believed that everyone is assigned by God to a certain vocation. The ideas of a fixed vocation for everyone and of an "intraworldly asceticism"—an asceticism that functions within the world, "but not of it," in distinction to monastic asceticism, which withdraws from the world—called for industriousness and moderation. Such ideals rejected a life of ease and luxury but did not require the standard of poverty implicit in the pattern of monastic life. Wesley's economic ethics, set forth in the sermon "On the Use of Money," appealed to the wealthy and the middle class and, at the same time, gave the working man a respectable place in society. As theologians have described Wesley's economic ethics, it "may seem an unwarranted baptism of free enterprise with the holy water of Christianity. At the least it looks [as though] . . . the Protestant spirit gives a moral sanction to capitalistic pursuits." (Waldo Beach and H. Richard Niebuhr, *Christian Ethics*, The Ronald Press Company, 1955, p. 363.)

As Wesley's life demonstrated, this kind of "capitalistic pursuit" does not preclude a concern for the welfare of our fellowman. Recognizing the tragic injustices brought on by the Industrial Revolution, Wesley tried to alleviate the bleak proverty of the lower classes by building schools, homes, and hospitals for the needy, the poor, and the sick. Concerned about the danger of abuses by the rich, he worked for the economic amelioration of those living in misery; he tried to salvage them from debtors' prisons and the grips of pawnbrokers. Wesley preached that the grace of God is available for all, the dispossessed as much as the opulent, and he claimed that to earn salvation it is not enough to live a moral private life but that such private righteousness must be combined with social concern. To this democratizing effect of Wesley's ethic is attributed the claim that Wesley saved England from the sort of revolution experienced by France.

Ethics and Economic Realities

Although Wesley and other religious leaders have had an important impact on economic activity within society, in modern times there has been an increasing separation between ethical ideals and economic policy and behavior. In the middle ages down at least to the middle of the sixteenth century, the fundamental assumption about the relationship between economic realities and moral attitudes was that economic activity should be subordinated to the traditional morality expounded by the church. Although the church itself was a highly organized financial institution, the social teaching of the church looked at commerce as a dangerous activity and at trade as an occupation that serves, according to Aquinas, "the lust of gain." It was Calvin who gave capital, credit, profit, and lawful, moderate interest respectability. This change was of momentous importance to the growth of capitalistic enterprise.

Calvin, although he accepted the realities of commercial transactions, stressed the superiority of moral law over economic expediency. The omnipotent church still enforced the standards of economic morality. Only at the end of the sixteenth century did signs of a divorce of economic realities from religious doctrines become evident. This divorce became a reality during the seventeenth and eighteenth centuries—the era of progress in economic thought, of growth in trade (described by a member of the British Parliament as the "fairest mistress in the world"), and of the recognition of economics as a subject for scientific study.

Private property was no longer regarded as a necessary evil but became one of the most important human rights, anterior to the existence of the State. Referring to this right, Locke argued that "the supreme power cannot take from any man any part of his property without his consent." The expansion of trade, the accumulation of wealth, and an irrespressible desire for economic gain were no longer sins denounced by saints and sages but became virtues leading to the conquest of the world. The deadly sin of avarice—committed when a man sought more wealth than was necessary for a livelihood in his state of life—now emerged as a virtue of social power and economic opulence.

The worship of wealth replaced the ethics expressed by St. Paul in his letter to Timothy: "Those who want to be rich fall into temptations and snares and many foolish harmful desires which plunge men into ruin and perdition. The love of money is the root of all evil things." (I Timothy 6:9-10.) Social responsibility, upon which religious teaching had insisted, was replaced by a new individualist morality subordinated to material interests and economic motives. The rise of purely economic criteria to evaluate human behavior led to an outburst of economic enterprise and of economic progress, but the new materialistic civilization was indifferent to the need for a just social order. This indifference led to the exploitation evidenced by the results of "laissez-faire laissez-aller" economic policies—and thus to recurrent revolts against the social order.

In order to avoid such social convulsions, we have to keep in mind that although economic efficiency is indispensable for the success of a businessman, such success cannot endure when it is divorced from moral considerations and when the businessman's activities violate the rights of his fellowman to self-respect and dignity. In the long run, what is morally wrong can never be economically fruitful, and no economic action can be sound without an accepted system of values. Expediency does not preclude the entrepreneur's concern for the welfare of his fellowman. It was Dr. Samuel Johnson who said that "a decent provision for the poor is a true test of civilization."

A deep understanding of the true meaning of life will lead the businessman to understand the evils of purely selfish desires and to realize the gain that can be obtained within the framework of his duty to serve others. Accepting social responsibility is not only an ethical precept but is also the wisdom and law of life. In order to succeed economically, the businessman has to channel his efforts, talents, energies, and intelligence into avenues that will lead the business to prosper. His efforts, however, must be combined with his responsibility for promoting the well-being of the society in which he lives and should give such responsibility priority over selfish desires for material gains. Adhering to such a principle of cooperation does not undermine the springs of free initiative—the cornerstone of business endeavor in a free society. This cooperation can be achieved without the rich becoming poorer.

The Entrepreneur—An Essential Factor in Production

The classic economists used to list three requisites of production: land, labor, and capital. (Production itself—one part of the traditional trilogy of production, distribution, and consumption—is defined as the creation of utility, which consists in increasing the desirability of an economic good; an economic factor is defined as anything that has an influence on production, distribution, or consumption.) Land, the starting point of all economic life, embraces all natural resources created without the assistance of labor. It comprises more than the earth's surface, for it includes oceans, rivers, mineral deposits, water power, trees in the virgin forests, and the fish in the river. Land without labor fails to have utility until human effort secures the desirability of the goods. By capital, we understand produced goods intended for use in further production; they do not gratify directly human wants. Examples are machines on a production line, typewriters in an office, and the truck used in transporting goods. (In commerce, "capital" is the word used for the money invested in a business.)

In modern economics, another distinct agent of production has been added to the three briefly described above: the entrepreneur. His function is primarily to guide the other three resources in the productive process—land, labor, and capital—and organize them into effective use. He determines the relation of land, labor, and capital in trying to obtain the greatest output for a given production. The profitability of a business endeavor depends upon his ability to organize the productive process and adjudge correctly the market and its wants. The function of the entrepreneur is to take risks and bear uncertainties. This is why it is sometimes argued that ownership, not management (salaried executives), is the distinguishing characteristic of the business enterprise.

American industry is highly concentrated because modern technology requires substantial capital investments for large-scale research and production and distribution facilities. (Concentration should not be confused with monopoly; even in an industry which is concentrated in the hands of a few independently acting companies there may well be effective competition.) In large corporate organizations, entrepreneurial decisions are delegated to management— employed executive officers. Since our discussion is concerned with decisions made on behalf of the business enterprise, there is no need to follow the distinction between management and ownership.

The entrepreneur constantly makes decisions which vary in scale (in proportion to the size of the business), in range, and in type. In order to recognize the main types of decisions, it would be helpful to disperse certain misconceptions and then outline the fundamental precepts which express the philosophy of freedom of enterprise and underlie the operation of a business enterprise in a free society. The first misconception we must guard against is identifying freedom of enterprise with the principle "Let the economy run itself." This in practice implies that private enterprise should be left entirely to itself. This principle, as history shows, leads to overgrown individualism, which can be transformed into injustice and exploitation. Some government restrictions are needed to prevent antisocial activities and to promote social welfare.

The second misconception is the assumption that freedom of enterprise is ordained by God and any limitation of this freedom should be considered as an attempt to undermine our political system or to subvert the religious foundations of this country. Nothing can drive men away from a belief in the free enterprise system so quickly as forcing upon them man-made dogmas that are asserted to be God-given truths. (See Andrew R. Cecil, "Dogmas and Moral Values," in *The Third Way*, The University of Texas at Dallas, 1979, pp. 23-40.)

The Rights to Private Property and to Profits

The economic philosophy known as the "free enterprise" or "private enterprise" system, although it places some restrictions on the businessman, offers him more modern freedom than any other business system in the world. In our mixed economy, which combines elements of laissez-faire, socialism (evidenced by governmental ownership, regulation, control, and taxation) and even syndicalism (evidenced by the role of labor and of other organized groups), the businessman is free to choose his business or occupation, to develop new products, to invent new methods, and to enter new markets. The characteristics of the "free enterprise" or capitalistic economy include freedom of contracts, the right of each individual enterprise to compete for the customer's favor under a system of prices determined by the interaction of the forces of supply and demand, and the right to private property and profits.

A. *Private Property*

James Madison, setting forth his constitutional concepts of "property and liberty," defined property as "that domination which one man claims and exercises over the external things of the world, in exclusion of

every other individual." Elaborating upon the meaning of property, he explained that "as a man is said to
have a right to his property, he may be equally said to
have property in his rights." Among the various rights
that should be protected by a "just government, which
impartially secures to every man whatever his own,"
he lists man's "property in the free use of his faculties
and free choice of the objects on which to employ
them." This "property in right" and the right to use
our faculties in a productive manner, translated into
the patent field, have a great impact on the economy
of our time, which is often described as the era of
technological revolution.

For the purpose of our discussion of the businessman's right to private property, let us single out the
"property in right" known as the right to invention or
the patent right. Vast and relatively new industries in
which the public has a direct concern are often the
products in large part of recent inventions covered by
patents. They include industries in the fields of com-
puters, communication, electronics, and aerospace, as
well as those based on major breakthroughs in the
petrochemical, pharmaceutical, and other phases of
applied chemistry, many of which are related to advances in human health and welfare.

In his dramatic account of the life and times of
Henry V of England, Shakespeare declaims through
one of his characters: "O! For a muse of fire that would
ascend the brightest heaven of invention." Abraham
Lincoln put his finger on the fuel that feeds the fire of
inventive genius. It is the patent system, which Lincoln proclaimed has added "the fuel of interest to the
fire of genius." (Cut in stone over the main entrance of

the United States Patent Office are Lincoln's words: "The Patent System Added the Fuel of Interest to the Fire of Genius".) Lincoln himself was a patentee.

Article 1 of the Constitution authorizes Congress to grant exclusive rights "to Authors and Inventors . . . to their respective Writings and Discoveries" in order to promote the "Progress of Science and Useful Arts." Patents are often characterized as governmentally created monopolies. Because of the people's intense aversion to monopolies those with antipatent attitudes will refer to "patent monopoly" to denote the derogation of public interest. Our jurisprudence makes a clear distinction between a monopoly, which takes from the public, and the right of the inventor, who deprives the public of nothing but gives something valuable to the people by contributing to the wealth of human knowledge.

The word "patent" denotes a beneficial grant to the growth and greatness of our nation. That this is the nature and purpose of our patent system was explained by Justice Roberts as follows:

"Though often so characterized a patent is not, accurately speaking, a monopoly, for it is not created by the executive authority at the expense and to the prejudice of all the community . . . The term 'monopoly' connotes the giving of an exclusive privilege for buying, selling, working, or using a thing which the public freely enjoyed prior to the grant. Thus a monopoly takes something from the people. An inventor deprives the public of nothing which it enjoyed before his discovery, but gives something of value to the community by adding to the sum of human knowledge." *(United States v. Dubilier Condenser Corporation,* 289 U.S. 178, 186, 53 S. Ct. 554, 557 [1933].)

The reward of sharing his ideas for the enrichment of human knowledge with the community is 'the inventor's right to control his inventions for seventeen years. This right is, as Chief Justice Marshall pointed out in 1832, "the reward stipulated for the advantage derived by the public for the exertions of the individual, and is intended as a stimulus to those exertions." *(Grant v. Raymond,* 6 Pet. 218, 241 [1832].)

Americans have an instinctive aversion to monopolies. As early as 1883, the Supreme Court stated that it was never the object of the patent laws to grant a "monopoly for every trifling device . . . Such an indiscriminate creation of exclusive privileges tends rather to obstruct than stimulate invention." *(Atlantic Works v. Brady,* 107 U.S. 192, 200, 2 S. Ct. 225, 231 [1883].) The subject matter, to be patentable, must transcend the ordinary level of skill in art. When the improvement, for instance, is just the work of the skillful mechanic, acquainted with the business, it lacks those degrees of skill and ingenuity which constitute essential elements of every invention.

The far-reaching social and economic consequences of a patent give the public a paramount interest in seeing that patent monopolies spring from backgrounds free from fraud or other inequitable conduct, and that such rights are kept within their legitimate scope. Only inventions and discoveries which further human knowledge and are new and useful justify the special inducement of the private patent monopoly. Ideas independent of the means to carry them out are not patentable. A patent, explained the Supreme Court, is not "a hunting license. It is not a reward for the search, but compensation for its successful conclusion." (*Brenner v. Manson,* 383 U.S. 519, 536, 86 S. Ct. 1033, 1042 [1966].) Consequently, patent "relates to the world of commerce rather than to the realm of philosophy."

Our industrial society, in undergoing the present technological revolution, can never lose sight of the fact that continuing industrial advancement is dependent upon an enormous outlay by business and industry for research and development. In 1983, Americans captured all four of the Nobel Prizes in science. Since the end of World War II, Americans have won 113 of the coveted awards in science, followed by Britain with thirty-eight, West Germany with thirteen, and France with six. This success should in large measure be attributed to the close ties between universities and industry, ties that do not exist in Europe. (See Diane L. Contu, "European Nations Fret Over Mounting Losses of Scientists to the U.S.," *Wall Street Journal,* October 21, 1983, p. 1.)

Since no individual or corporation may be expected to provide investment in research and development without the prospect of a fair return on such capital outlay, a dependable incentive must be relied upon. No better incentive for private industry had been devised than the patent system, which gives the inventor a monopoly on what he has discovered so that no one else shall make or use or sell his inventions without his permission. This right to property, known as the patent, nourishes and fires the flame that brings quality to our standards of living.

B. *The Right to Profits*

The high degree of business efficiency experienced in a free enterprise economy may be attributed to the desire for economic and pecuniary gain. The profit motive provides incentives for business performance. There are those who regard the profits of the business-man with the same disfavor with which they view the interest received by the capitalist. Provided that profit reflects not monoply power but a service to society, condemnation of profits is the result of failure to appreciate their role in impelling the entrepreneurs to discover and experiment with new products and im-proved methods and processes which contribute to economic progress. Without profit there would be no accumulation of wealth, which is indispensable for economic growth—accomplished only by launching into the speculative and the untried. Such ventures entail risk.

The hope for profit induces the businessman to undertake leadership and to risk his capital and the capital entrusted to him by others because of his abili-ties and good judgment concerning other people's needs and wants. Profit is justly called the mainspring of the free enterprise mechanism. When the profit motive is destroyed, the free enterprise economy is destroyed, and government undertakes the function of the entrepreneur in a totalitarian economy. This usurpation results in empty shelves in stores, a constant feeling of hunger in the populace, and a general harshness of life. When the State assumes control of the economy, it robs the people in order to build a mighty police and military machine and to provide an abundant life for the members of the ruling party. A free economy relies upon the profit motive that stirs productivity. Substitutes like the planned economy offered by a police state prove to be unproductive.

In the Soviet Union, where the economy is planned and the laws of supply and demand do not operate, planners and economists (to mention only the economic planner N. A. Voznesensky, who was executed in 1950, and the prominent economist E.G. Liberman) have suggested that the distressing conditions of the Soviet economy could be alleviated by accepting profit as an essential factor in obtaining efficiency in any enterprise. Providing incentives for managers, giving increased authority to directors, and leaving profits to the disposal of individual enterprise should improve the constantly declining growth in the Soviet Union's economy, assert concerned Soviet economists. These suggestions have always been rejected as political heresy in conflict with the monopoly power of the ruling communist party.

In the satellite countries of Eastern Europe, under the watchful eye of the Soviet Union, attempts have been made at economic reform. According to press reports, in Hungary in 1983, for instance, the maximum number of employees allowed in a private business was raised from six to twelve; in State industries, emphasis on profits has replaced emphasis on volume, the decisionmaking powers of plant managers have been increased, and bonuses tied to performance have been introduced. These economic reforms, unique in Eastern Europe, were made in the realization that profits are made only if consumers are provided with something they want at a reasonable price and that no political indoctrination can change this economic truth. These experiments for carrying out this truth, aimed at economic improvement, may, however, disappear at any time with a new wave of purges and a subsequent restoration of the discredited policies of the planned economy.

In China, the supreme leader, Deng Xiaoping— denounced almost two decades ago by Maoist zealots in Peking as a "capitalist roader"—has embarked on a dramatic kind of revolution in his country's economy. In his efforts to rebuild China's economy, laid waste by twenty years of Maoist experimentation, Deng in 1978 dismantled collectivized agriculture by restoring family farms and by permitting peasants, once they turned over a relatively modest quota of their corps to the government, to sell the rest on the open market. The results of restoring free-market incentives to the rural population of 800 million have been astounding; production has soared and the prosperity of the peasants has boomed.

In October 1984, the 618 delegates to the Third Plenum of the Twelfth Central Committee adopted a resolution outlining new economic reforms aimed at Chinese industry, which has continued to stagnate. The changes adopted permit more goods to fluctuate according to the law of supply and demand, with prices responding to market forces. Factory managers have been allowed to fire workers at their discretion and to set wage differentials among employees, thus eliminating the guarantees to industrial workers of employment for life and the long held commitment to egalitarianism. This new incentive system was introduced because—as the 16,000 word document announcing the radical new schemes for economic growth declares—"socialism does not mean pauperism, for it aims at the elimination of poverty." Deng, who inspired the new scheme aimed at invigorating sluggish industries and at offering urban workers the fruits of free enterprise, turned Marx's dictum "From each according to his abilities, to each according to his needs" into "to each according to his work and merits." The astounding success of Japan, South Korea, Taiwan, Singapore, and Hong Kong gives convincing evidence in favor of a private enterprise path to prosperity which wipes out economic stagnation and misery.

The freedom of individuals to pursue their own economic interests does not mean that all business decisions should be dominated by unrestrained individualism. Such individualsim has produced a more advanced as well as a more opulent society than any other economic system, but it also carries the perils of possession-centeredness and self-righteousness. Economic self-interest provides a stimulus for resourcefulness, ingenuity, and inventiveness, but business enterprise has also a great responsibility to the community in which it operates. Business decisions of an economic character cannot be separated from their social implications. It is essential for the well-being of a society that business leadership provides a healthy combination of self-interest and an awareness of the public interest when it makes its decisions.

Economic Decisions

One may roughly divide the economic decisions an entrepreneur makes into those of an internal economic character and those of a social nature. The first include organizational and operational decisions which vary with each enterprise, such as what products or services to offer, what prices to charge, what methods of marketing and advertising to use, and what capital market to approach for equity and loan capital. Regardless of the kind of enterprise, these decisions should be guided by respect for the individual employees, good service to customers, and the pursuit of excellence. Our discussion is limited to economic decisions of a social nature which are concerned with the expectations of the public at large and of communities from business management. To meet these expectations is a part of the broad spectrum of management responsibility that includes the active role it plays in influencing human values as well as influencing the economic and political life of the society in which the business operates. The preservation of economic freedom, one of many interrelated freedoms guaranteed by the Constitution, depends on the ethical norms and the public spirit that guide economic decisions. Because of this interrelation, it cannot be

separated from the other freedoms enjoyed under a
constitutional government.

A. *Free Competition and the Consumer*

In the free enterprise system, there is competition
among the suppliers, on the one hand, and the buyers,
on the other, in the market for goods and services.
Competition among buyers will cause prices to go up if
some buyers fail to satisfy their demand at current
prices. Competition among suppliers will cause prices
to go down until the price established by them
through bidding against each other enables everyone
willing to sell at that price to do so. When a supplier
gains a monopoly through mergers, the purchase of
rival companies, or other ways, in his position as the
only source of supply he will offer for sale the quantity
of goods that will permit him to obtain the highest
price and to maximize his profits. Conspiracies among
competing sellers to limit production, divide markets,
or fix prices (sometimes called "gentlemen's agreements") have for their purpose the manipulation of the
market price in isolation from the essential conditions
of competition. Such unfair or deceptive acts or practices in commerce evoke legislative or judicial action
to protect the consumer deprived of the benefits of
free competition.

Monopolies are odious and a threat to the social
interest because such predatory policies enhance the
prices of the articles monopolized, cause the quality of
a commodity or service to which the monopoly relates
to deteriorate, and often deprive persons who other-

wise would be employed of their means of livelihood. The resulting imbalance of economic power is followed by an imbalance of political power that may undermine the foundations of economic freedom.

Maintaining a free economy requires us to accept the truths that a person desires to profit from trade and commerce and that profit should be ensured by free competition. Faith in the value of competition and in the material reward known as profit is the heart of our national economic policy. The businessman who engages in competition with the object of gaining this reward is required to conform to rules that protect the interest of the consumer and the survival of smaller competitors. The antitrust laws provide these competitive rules.

From this country's beginning there has been an abiding and widespread fear of the evils which flow from concentration of economic power in the hands of few—that is, from monopoly. In the words of James Madison: "The truth is that all men having power ought to be mistrusted." Even Adam Smith was aware of the threat of big business to the free play of market prices when he observed that "people of the same trade seldom meet together, even for merriment and diversion, but the conversation ends in a conspiracy against the public, or in some contrivance to raise prices." Selfishness uncontrolled by competition disregards the interest of the consumer, dampens individual initiative, and obstructs the course of trade.

During the Civil War the demands created by the government in the war effort spurred economic concentration and increased the ability of manufacturers to offer speedy production. Upon the cessation of hostilities, the growing tendency of powerful business combinations to restrain competition resulted in the elimination of smaller businessmen through monopolistic pressures. As a result, in 1890 the Congress passed the Sherman Act. This was a time when many felt that the nation had to be set free from the "insidious menace inherent in large aggregations of capital, particularly when held by corporations." (*Liggett Co. v. Lee*, 288 U.S. 517, 549, 53 S. Ct. 481, 490 [1933].) In his decision on the *Standard Oil* case, Justice Harlan recreated the period for us when he wrote:

> "All who recall the condition of the country in 1890 will remember that there was everywhere, among the people gnerally, a deep feeling of unrest. The Nation had been rid of human slavery— fortunately, as all now feel—but the conviction was universal that the country was in real danger from another kind of slavery sought to be fastened on the American people; namely, the slavery that would result from aggregations of capital in the hands of a few individuals and corporations controlling, for their own profit and advantage exclusively, the entire business of the country, including the production and sale of the necessaries of life." (*Standard Oil Co. of New Jersey v. United States*, 221 U.S. 1, 83, 31 S. Ct. 502, 525 [1911].)

The purpose of the Sherman Act is to prohibit monopolies, contracts, and combinations which would unduly restrain trade and commerce. The courts have described the Sherman Act as "the Magna Charta of

free enterprise" designed to be a comprehensive charter of economic liberty aimed at preserving free and
unfettered competition as the rule of trade. In fact, the
Sherman Act did not break new ground but had its
genesis in the English common law doctrine that competition is the "life of trade." The significance of this
doctrine of the legal import of "restraint of trade" was
declared again and again in the decisions of English
courts before and after the date of our independence.
In France as early as in the fifteenth century, price
fixing and monopolization were punishable by the loss
of property in perpetuity and by exile.

The Sherman Act, explained Justice Black, "rests on
the premise that the unrestrained interaction of competitive forces will yield the best allocation of our
economic resources, the lowest prices, the highest
quality and the greatest material progress, which at
the same time providing an environment conducive to
the preservation of our democratic political and social
institutions." (*Northern Pacific Railway v. United
States*, 356 U.S. 1, 4, 78 S. Ct. 514, 517 [1958].)

Although the Sherman Act was passed in response
to an irresistible tide of public opinion (it passed both
houses of Congress with only one dissenting vote), the
Act failed to protect the small businessman from
elimination through the monopolistic pressures of
large combinations which used mergers to grow even
more powerful. It was not a preventive law against
incipient abuse and dealt only with accomplished
facts. The rule of reason adopted by the Court in the
Standard Oil case of 1911, which provided that only
"unreasonable" restraints of trade were forbidden,

rendered this Act general and too vague. Further-more, in the *United States Steel* case (251 U.S. 417, 451, 40 S. Ct. 293, 299 [1920]) and the *International Harvester* case (274 U.S. 693, 708, 47 S. Ct. 748, 753 [1927]), the Court enhanced the proposition that the law does not make the mere size of corporation, however impressive, an offense when unaccompanied by unlawful conduct in the exercise of its power. The effect of these decisions and of the "rule of reason" was an accelerated pattern of mergers and a concentration of power which resulted in injurious and destructive business practices.

As a result, in 1914 came the enactment of the Clayton Act and of the Federal Trade Commission Act. In Section 7 of the former, Congress prohibited corporations under most circumstances from merging by purchasing the stock of their competitors. The Federal Trade Commission Act outlawed "unfair methods" of competition in commerce. When busi-nessmen found a way to avoid Section 7 of the Clayton Act and merged simply by purchasing their rival's assets, driving small businessmen out of the market, Congress in 1950 amended Section 7 and broadened its scope by passing the Celler-Kefauver Anti-Merger Act.

The purpose of the amendment was to clamp down on the merger movement, in which large corporations had been buying out small companies, and to arrest the steady erosion of small independent business in our economy.

This enactment was not directed against all mergers; it only prohibited mergers the effect of which

"may be to substantially lessen competition or to tend
to create a monopoly." The 1950 amendment was
addressed against the danger of the erosion of competition through the cumulative effect of acquisitions by
large corporations, none of which by itself might be
sufficient to constitute a violation of the Sherman Act.

The revitalized Section 7 of the Clayton Act was
concerned not only with the actual effect of a merger,
but also with its effect upon future competition. There
is a distinction between actual and reasonably probable competitive effects. While the Sherman Act is
violated only when substantial adverse competitive
effects have been proved, the Clayton Act arrests a
trend toward centralization in its incipiency before
that trend develops to the point that a market is left in
the grip of a monopoly. The standard for measuring
the substantiality of the effect of a merger on competition is that of a "reasonable probability" of lessening
competition. That standard is more lenient than that of
"a certainty" on the one hand, but more stringent than
that of a "mere possibility" on the other.

The history of legislation aimed at reaching practices considered dangerous to trade and commerce
includes numerous laws, among them the statutes
against price discrimination (Section 2 of the Clayton
Act, amended in 1936 by the Robinson-Patman Act),
which curb the buying power of buyers who demand
price and other concessions not available to others;
against some interlocking directorates (Section 8 of the
Clayton Act), which forbid corporations to have the
same director if such corporations are competitors and
in which agreement for elimination of competition

between them would be illegal; against unfair methods of competition and of unethical conduct (the 1914 Federal Trade Commission Act); against false advertising of food, drugs, therapeutic devices, and cosmetics (the 1938 Wheeler-Lea Act, which amended the Federal Trade Commission Act); and others enacted to advance public faith in the value of competition, to protect the welfare of the consumer, and to prevent monopolies.

It may be noted that antitrust legislation did not seek to break up large corporations, although some prominent scholars and jurists, including Justice Brandeis, spoke of huge concerns as "the negation of industrial democracy." The changes caused by the dispersed ownership of corporate shares and the concentration of power in the hands of a few, Justice Brandeis maintained, are so fundamenal and far reaching as to lead "scholars to compare the 'evolving corporate system' with the feudal system; and to lead other men of insight and experience to assert that this 'master institution of civilized life' is committing it to the rule of plutocracy." (*Liggett v. Lee,* 288 U.S. 517, 565, 566, 53 S. Ct. 481, 496 [1933].)

The same fears have been expressed in the Congress. Remarked Representative Emanuel Celler: "Small independent decentralized business of the kind that built up our country, of the kind that made our country great, first, is fast disappearing, and second, is being made dependent upon monster concentration." (95 Cong. Rec. 11486.) Asked Senator Kefauver: "Shall we permit the economy of the country to gravitate into the hands of a few corporations . . .? Or on the other hand are we going to preserve small business, local operations, and free enterprise?" (96 Cong. Rec. 16450.)

The trend toward greater concentration continues to grow. Bigness, however, does not always imply monopoly. Companies may become big by serving their customers successfully and not by taking advantage of them. In highly industrialized countries, an industry may be dominated by a few big firms locked in fierce competition for domestic and global markets. Technological advances and large-scale production demand expensive research, capital for expansion, efficient production, and aggressive sales promotion. The goals of ever-expanding production and of offering the product at competitive prices can in certain industries be achieved only by large corporations aggressively competing with each other.

Mature large companies engaged in competitive struggle are not necessarily inimical to the public welfare, and their managers are not necessarily indifferent to the effects of their decisions upon the total economy and on society. International (or multinational) corporations have become a necessity. As Britain's Arnold Toynbee pointed out, "Sovereignty on a local scale is an illusion because you can't be economically independent locally." ("As I See It," *Forbes Magazine*, April 15, 1974, p. 68.) Each of the 157 so-called sovereign States is dependent upon the rest of the world for raw materials and sometimes for food itself in order to live.

Because foreign producers are not governed by our antitrust rules, they can combine with their governments' encouragement and form competitive units of maximum efficiency, whereas American manufacturers are inhibited by the antitrust laws. This not only affects the ability of American industries to compete with foreign manufacturers in international markets, but also very seriously affects our ability to resist the penetration of many of our key domestic markets by foreign competition. At the time when the laws were drawn, the business world did not face the present problems which make international trade so hazardous. In order to increase the ability of our industries to battle foreign competition stimulated by foreign governments, efforts to liberalize these laws should be encouraged through such measures as special tax incentives, antitrust exceptions, low-cost credit, and protection from imports and foreign takeovers. The antitrust statutes must be related to the present realities of fierce foreign competition.

B. *Stockholders' Expectations*

The limited liability offered by corporations contributes greatly to their growth. Because of this growth, complete disclosure and adequate accounting have become important responsibilities of management toward stockholders and the public. In the absence of some type of governmental control over transactions, unscrupulous issuers and dealers may defraud uninformed, naive purchasers. The protection of the public against the possibility of fraud demanded legislation. In the United States, the initial attempts to institute governmental control were made at the state

level. (The first general securities law was enacted by
the State of Kansas in 1911.)

State securities acts are commonly referred to as
"blue sky laws." These statutes were initially aimed at
speculative schemes to sell securities that were backed
by nothing more substantial than so many feet of blue
sky, and this description has had a lasting influence.
The blue sky laws were designed to protect members
of the public from becoming the prey of promoters of
worthless securities in fly-by-night concerns, visionary
oil wells, distant gold mines, and other fraudulent
exploitations. The blue sky laws differ from state to
state, but they comprise one purpose—the general
welfare and the protection of the public from deceit
and fraud in securities transactions.

As part of the aftermath of the crash of 1929 and the
depression of the 1930s, the Congress passed the
Securities Act of 1933 and the Securities Exchange Act
of 1934 in order to achieve a high standard of business
ethics in the securities industry. The Securities Act of
1933 was designed to provide investors with full disclosure of material information concerning public
offerings of securities in commerce, to protect investors against fraud, and—partly through the imposition of specified civil liabilities—to promote ethical
standards of honesty and fair dealing. "Publicity,"
stated Justice Brandeis, "is justly commendable as a
remedy for social and industrial disease. Sunlight is
said to be the best disinfectant." The 1934 Act was
intended principally to protect investors against the
manipulation of stock prices through regulation of
transactions upon securities exchanges and in over-

the-counter markets and to impose regular reporting requirements on companies whose stocks are listed on national securities exchanges. As part of the 1934 Act, Congress created the Securities and Exchange Commission, which is provided with an arsenal of flexible enforcement powers.

Protection of the investor was not the sole purpose of the federal securities regulations. Their objectives were also to protect the integrity of the American securities market, to restore the confidence of the public in sound securities markets, and to bring available capital into productive channels. Investors make up a very large segment of the population, since pension plans, insurance programs, and mutual funds, with all their beneficiaries, have many working assets in stock market securities. If investors are not confident that the market is fair and hospitable to them, they will question the very wisdom of investing in equities. The necessity of protecting the interests of the investors parallels industry's abilities to raise the required capital and to mobilize it for productive purposes. The regulations are designed to protect the investing public but also to protect honest corporate business. The state blue sky laws remain valid so long as they do not conflict with federal securities acts.

The basic means by which the Securities Act attempts to accomplish its purpose of protecting the investing public is the requirement by the Act of full and fair disclosure. Prior to the issuance of a security, the issuer must file with the Securities and Exchange Commission a registration statement containing certain information with respect to the security, its

issuer, and its underwriters. The law further requires
that buyers be provided with a prospectus containing
all essential information, which must be included in
the registration statement. Material misstatements or
omissions pertaining to the issuance of a security are
causes for subjecting the issuer to criminal or civil
sanctions.

Congress recognized that insiders may have access
to information about their corporations not available to
the rest of the investing public. By trading on this
information, these persons could reap profits at the
expense of less well-informed investors. To "curb the
evils of insider trading" and to prevent the unfair use
of information which may have been obtained by directors, officers, and beneficial owners by reason of
their relationship to the issuer, Congress in Section
16(b) of the Act enacted a flat rule that a corporation
(or its shareholders acting for it) could recover the
profits these insiders made on short-swing security
transactions (purchases and sales within six months of
each other). From Section 10(b) (a general antifraud
provision), the SEC and the courts have fashioned
another prohibition on insiders using nonpublic information in even a single transaction.

Reaping profits at the expense of stockholders does
not merely violate the Securities Acts. Extreme practices of executive compensation and excessive retire-
ment benefits may also undermine the moral integrity
of the business organization. Theodore V. Houser, the
Chairman of Sears, Roebuck and Company, wrote:

"The service of great educators, great scientists,
great public servants are equally invaluable to the

country. Such services are not put exclusively or even primarily on a cash basis. If we sincerely believe that the publicly-owned American corporation is the most efficient and most desirable means of serving the material and, to some extent, the cultural needs of the people, then those endowed with the ability to lead these great organizations should begin to conceive of their remuneration partly in terms of the satisfaction of making a real contribution to national progress." (*Big Business and Human Values*, McGraw Hill Book Company, Inc., 1957, pp. 27-28.)

The lavish raises in executive salaries in 1984, a year of economic recovery, were assailed by management experts, union leaders, and rank-and-file employees. Critics, concerned that "excessive" executive salaries could spark a demand for higher wages on down the line and thus make U.S. industry less competitive with foreign products, called for setting up legislative restrictions if companies failed to control salaries by voluntary curbs. Chrysler Corporation's Chairman, Lee Iacocca, criticized the bonuses paid to top executives of auto producers by describing them as "scandalous." He warned: "You reach a point of asking how high is up. How high is tolerable in a publicly held company? . . . We as an industry had better start acting responsibly." In response to Mr. Iacocca's criticism, a General Motors official noted that in addition to generous stock options the Chrysler Chairman was promised a gift of 150,000 common shares valued at about $3.75 million if he stayed with the company. (*The Wall Street Journal*, May 17, 1984, p. 19.)

Suggestions have been made to remedy these criticisms: to limit top salaries to amounts no more than 25 times of the lowest paid employee of a company; to prohibit salaries larger than that of the President of the United States; to correlate salaries with a company's performance over several years rather than just with annual profits; or to require shareholder approval of executive contracts. (The Securities and Exchange Commission has recommended new rules requiring shareholder approval of the so-called "golden parachutes" offered executives of corporations that have been taken over.) The arguments that television personalities, actors, and athletes earn more than business executives and that the pay of each executive is based not only on his skill and vision but also on such factors as the size of the company, its performance, and the responsibilities of the individual executive within it miss the main point—that businessmen should conceive of their remuneration partly in terms of making a contribution to the prosperity of their country.

While the public justly may expect a change in the emphasis placed on the monetary compensation of executives with outstanding leadership capacity, a change in the pattern of the conduct of stockholders would also add appreciably to the stature of corporations and their real contribution to national progress. The quick turnover of shares in the stock market and the wide fluctuation in their quotations evidence the fact that some owners of the shares have a speculative interest in the stock rather than an interest in making a corporate investment. From these daily gyrations, no objective economic indices can be extracted since they only reflect the impalpable, unpredictable play of the market.

Crosscurrents

Along with his responsibilities toward customers and shareholders, the businessman, in order to preserve his position of stewardship, has to discharge his social responsibilities. His success or failure in discharging the latter responsibilities is judged in terms of the public interest, which demands that individual self-interest and society's interest become mutually compatible. The history of "society's interest" is the story of crosscurrents that have resulted in a long series of more or less successful reforms and legislation. Already in the writings of the Founders of our nation we may find these crosscurrents at work in devising the economic and social structure of this country. The crosscurrents result from a cluster of ideas that have attempted to satisfy the public interest and the demands of special interest groups at the same time. To serve self-interest and the general interest, they tried, as Pelatiah Webster (1725-1795)—a publicist and Philadelphia businessman—expressed it, "to unite and combine" public and private actions so they will "mutually support, feed and quicken each other."

Fifteen centuries after Clement of Alexandria, who, as we described above, defended the institution of wealth as a source of relief for the hungry, homeless, and destitute, Noah Webster (1758-1843)—lexicographer, prominent lawyer, and author of

numerous books on political and scientific subjects—
asked in his letter to Daniel Webster: "What would
become of the poor without the rich? How would they
subsist without employment, and how could they be
employed without the capital of the rich? Who but the
wealthy can pay the public expenses?" Daniel Webster lent his support to the ideas of Alexander Hamilton, who favored the idea that wealthy citizens be
accorded a wide measure of governmental responsibility in order to ensure good government. In his concern that self-interest and the unreasonable demands
of interest groups might infringe on the well-being of
society, he warned that "selfishness which excludes
others from a participation of benefits" leads to self-
ruin.

Hamilton, who maintained that "equality is nonsense" and favored "propertied interests" in his concern to promote the general interest, proclaimed that
"liberty is freedom to acquire and keep wealth" and
that "the door ought to be equally open to all." John
Adams believed that in any society, which consists
inevitably of particians and plebeians, power should
be accorded to owners of property. Property, he
argued, breeds responsibility, and property owners
should serve as guardians of stability in government.
Yet we can find an ethical overtone in the fears he
expressed that the wellborn and the rich might become a closed tyrannical ruling class and in his idea
that to safeguard the general welfare "property must
be relatively widespread."

Madison, a passionate defender of private property,
also expected that the primary policy of legislation
should be to "reduce extreme wealth toward a state of

mediocrity, and to raise extreme indigence toward a state of comfort." Jefferson, bluntly rejecting the social dualism of an aristocracy and the common people, of rich and poor, of educated and illiterate, bitterly attacked Hamilton's concept of government by the elite and John Adams' argument in favor of a "national aristocracy." He was convinced that "here in America, through the instrumentality of political democracy, the lot of common men should somehow be made better" and that the government should intervene properly to protect the welfare of the citizens through democratic institutions. He shared, however, the view of conservative Federalists that "enterprise thrives best when left to individual initiative."

Conflicts must arise when each of the sectors of the economy—industry, agriculture, finance, and labor— is trying to advance its self-interest by seeking favors from government, frequently at the expense of the other sectors. The self-interest groups make it difficult to obtain a democratic consensus or to compromise competing interests. No policies can satisfy all political or social demands of all the economic sectors at the same time unless they realize that socially irrespons- ible action simply does not pay and that the sole purpose of their existence is to serve the society in general.

Current Trends

When we glance at the movement of thought in the area of economic life within the current century, we can observe that the cross trends turned into trends of growing emphasis on governmental authority. The accelerated governmental responsibility for social welfare programs and the dramatic changes in the extent of governmental interference in economic life that occurred within only seven decades are illustrated by the following excerpts from two messages to Congress. The first one came from President Grover Cleveland on February 16, 1887:

"I do not believe that the power and duty of the General Government ought to be extended to the relief of individual suffering which is in no matter properly related to the public service or benefit. A prevalent tendency to disregard the limited mission of this power and duty should, I think, be steadfastly resisted, to the end that the lesson should be constantly enforced that though the people support the Government, the Government should not support the people."

The second message was sent by President Dwight D. Eisenhower on January 14, 1954:

"The human problems of individual citizens are a proper and important concern of our Government. One such problem that faces every individual is the provision of economic security for his old age and economic security for his family in the event of his death. To help individuals provide for that security—to reduce both the fear and the incidence of destitution to the minimum—to promote the confidence of every individual in the future—these are proper aims of all levels of government, including the federal Government."

The spectacular increase of governmental services in the twentieth century reflects the growing public demand for the expansion of public education; for better quality schools and better trained teachers; for more adequate provisions for the poor, the aged, the unemployed, and the infirm; for better equiped hospitals and recreational facilities; for more public safety; for better roads, sanitation, and water supply; for social insurance; for farm-price supports; for safety codes; for public housing; for minimum wage laws; and for other services stemming from the progressing scope of governmental intervention in economic life.

Problems related to the economic order cannot be kept separate from sociopolitical problems. To avoid such a separation, the Federal Republic of Germany after World War II attempted to develop an economic system known as the "social market economy." "Market economy" means a decentralized economic system with the free play of market forces in which planning and decisionmaking rest in the hands of entrepreneurs. A "market economy" underpins freedom and is based on a well-functioning system of competition. The term "social" here is primarily to be understood as the intention to safeguard society against excessive concentration of economic power and as the assertion of the right of the government to adjust the undesirable results produced by the free market process.

Pursuing the goals of the "social market economy" in Germany, economic controls were abolished, seven million jobs were created between 1950 and 1970, and the increase of the real gross national product was followed by an expansion of external trade and a successful fight against inflation. In the social sphere, the broadening of the income-pyramid gave industrious people the chance to work their way up, thus providing greater social mobility. The Works Constitution Act introduced the system of worker participation, known as "codetermination," in order to give employees a share of responsibility for company decisions. The purpose of the involvement of workers in the decisionmaking process was to reduce the possibilities of employer/employee conflicts. For the same purpose, social legislation offered workers protection from dismissal, unemployment insurance, continued payment of wages for workers in the event of illness, new pension programs, measures for the protection of tenants, and a variety of other social reforms.

To summarize, the concept of a "social market economy" tried to link progress in the economy to success in the field of social reform. History, however, teaches us that no economic system is complete, because there will always be a tension between concept and reality, between the ideal and its working out in life. Such tensions cannot be removed or regulated by legislation, because no legal or social system is perfect. After three decades of growth, the postwar European economy—including that of West Germany—became stagnant. Economists blame this decline on too much attention to the "social part" and very little attention to the "market economy." They see the cause of the stagnant economy in the lavish welfare programs that could not be sustained and in the spiraling claims by every group within society to the right to get more each year—more pay, more fringe benefits, more job security.

Throughout the Free World, this century is also marked by the growing number of special interest groups: corporate organizations, chambers of commerce, labor unions, manufacturers' associations, churches, universities, foundations, minority groups, women's rights groups, environmentalists, and numerous others, all seeking the assistance of the supercolossal wizard—the government. The "omnipotent" government is expected to provide everything that anybody ever wanted and to be blamed for everything that anybody could not get. Lobbyists representing special interest groups have become a permanent part of the Washington scene. They plead their cases in the halls of Congress and before the agencies and departments of the Federal Government.

A government unconstrained by constitutional provisions becomes powerful enough to destroy a free society; this destruction would offer no escape for the special interest groups seeking favors at the expense of others. An unbounded government leads to communism and tyranny. The Nobel laureate Friedrich Hayek reminded us that "If we knew how freedom would be used, the case for it would largely disappear." In judging the contest between our mixed economy and communism, we are reminded of the legend of a Roman emperor who served as a judge of two singers. Upon hearing the first singer, he awarded the prize to the second singer without giving him a chance to perform. When asked for the reason for his hasty decision, he explained that he granted the prize on the grounds that no one could do worse than the first singer.

When we witness the endless misery brought by communist governments which instead of offering decent standards of living keep paddling in the mud of their falsehoods—the prize will be awarded without need of further scrutiny to a system enhancing economic freedom. It is up to the stewardship of the free entrepreneur to continue to deserve this prize. It is up to the free entrepreneur to realize that economic freedom does not mean exaltation of the profit motive over respect for human dignity. Free or private enterprise does not mean irresponsible concentration of power but a sense of justice, self-discipline, honesty, and firm ethical and moral norms.

The decisions and actions of the businessman affect the lives of many. Added together, the decisions of businessmen may in a certain measure determine the economic progress of a nation. The entrepreneur in a free economy should apply the principles of moral behavior in private life to his dealings with the public. Public morality cannot be divorced from private morality, and economic freedom does not justify ruthless pursuit of predatory self-interest. Fairness and moderation on the part of the free entrepreneur must support the moral structure upon which capitalism is built and which is indispensable for its survival.

LABOR IN A FREE SOCIETY

by

Ray Marshall

Ray Marshall

Professor Marshall, a native of Louisiana, earned his B.A. from Millsaps College, his M.A. from Louisiana State University, and his Ph.D. from the University of California at Berkeley. Since 1981 he has been Bernard Rapoport Centennial Professor of Economics and Public Affairs at The University of Texas at Austin. He previously served on the faculty of a number of American universities, including the University of Mississippi, Louisiana State University, and the University of Kentucky.

From 1977 to 1981 he was Secretary of Labor. As President Carter's chief advisor on labor matters, Mr. Marshall was responsible for carrying out the Department of Labor's mission "to foster, promote, and develop the welfare of the wage earners of the United States, to improve their working conditions, and to advance their opportunities for profitable employment." In carrying out these duties, he administered laws and programs in such areas as employment and training, labor statistics, labor-management relations, and other matters affecting the nation's expanding work force.

Professor Marshall has served on many boards and commissions, and is presently President of the National Policy Exchange and a member of the Steering Committee of the Economic Policy Council of the United Nations Association. He is Chairman of the Texas Job Training Coordinating Committee and a member of the Governor's Task Force on Immigration.

The author of numerous books and articles, Professor Marshall numbers among his most recent books Lagging Productivity Growth in the United States: Lessons from Abroad *(with Diane Werneke and Arvil V. Adams),* An Economic Strategy for the 1980s, *and* Labor Economics: Wages, Employment, and Trade Unionism *(with Allan G. King and Vernon M. Briggs, Jr.).*

LABOR IN A FREE SOCIETY

by

Ray Marshall

The subject of these lectures, moral values in a free society, is extremely important for individuals, institutions, and countries. Andrew Cecil put it well when he said: "At the heart of preserving our civilization is the recognition that the civilization which we represent cannot survive materially unless it is redeemed spiritually."

Let me say at the outset, however, that a concern for spiritual things does not come easily to one who is trained in the "dismal science" of economics. Orthodox economics in the United States is mainly concerned with material wealth, prices, quantities, markets, and money. Moreover, orthodox economics assumes that people are motivated mainly by their material self-interest—personal satisfaction, profits, etc. Most economists know these assumptions about human motivations are abstractions which must be modified when making political or personal decisions, but believe the abstractions serve useful intellectual purposes. Unfortunately, economists sometimes cause trouble when their preoccupation with quantification and abstractions causes them to confuse their models with reality. In the real world, categories that cannot be measured have a very strong impact on economic affairs; quality, equity, dignity, national pride, or humiliation all clearly have been powerful forces.

The material advantages of a free society are fairly obvious. Indeed, the Communists have pretty well lost the ideological conflict—almost no industrialized country on earth, not even others in its sphere of influence, seeks to emulate the Soviet Union. While some of the Third World countries are attempting other forms of centralized planning, none of them has demonstrated the economic vitality of a market economy. This has been dramatically revealed by the almost universal superior performance of the industrialized democracies of Western Europe and Japan.

The main weakness of the industrial market economies is their failure to emphasize adequately the *moral* underpinning of a free and democratic system. By our inconsistencies and failure to follow our own moral precepts, we too often permit the enemies of democracy to seize the moral high ground and put us on the defensive. We frequently appear to make abstractions of human suffering and ignore the moral imperatives of justice for the vulnerable at home and abroad. We weaken our case by focusing on the enemies of democracy, and even supporting many of them, rather than on the unjust conditions which nourish antidemocratic forces. This is tragic because in the end these moral considerations are likely to be much stronger than military or economic might. This tragedy is all the more unfortunate because of the moral superiority of a democratic society which is faithful to its basic principles. "A free society is a society with established values of respect for the dignity and worth of our fellowman, of concern for self-realization, and of appreciation for the imperatives of justice." (Andrew Cecil, *The Foundations of a Free Society*, U.T. Dallas, 1983, p. 21.) Our ability to be a force for justice is therefore a basic test of the viability of a free society.

Translated into the economic concerns of workers, a free society requires that we respect the dignity of work and the right of self-realization by workers. Work is earning a living, but it is more. With the growing participation of women in the work force, paid work is the way most adults identify themselves, organize their lives, and participate in the human community. The quality of work clearly has an important influence on the quality of all of our lives. By the same token unemployment—which seems to be ratcheting up with each succeeding recession—not only denies people the opportunity to earn a living, but also denies them the opportunity to contribute to the community. This is one of the reasons unemployment produces stress and guilt feelings by the unemployed and is highly correlated with such social pathologies as alcoholism, divorce, child abuse, suicide, and even infant mortality. Similarly, authoritarian and degrading work environments which assume that workers have only brawn to offer will rarely produce quality outcomes.

Economic justice therefore requires that we reexamine our attitudes about workers and nonworkers. We should strive for a society where all who are willing and able to work have incentives and opportunities to do so. We should also strive for dignity and equity in the work place in terms of opportunity for participation and advancement, compensation and participation in work decisions.

Free worker participation in the work place and in the larger society requires that workers have independent power sources to protect their interests and assure that their full and honest participation will not jeopardize their jobs. This means they must have the right to organize and bargain collectively through representatives of their own choosing, and that the benefits and costs of economic change be equitably shared. Indeed, to paraphrase Franklin Roosevelt, we are not likely to have a free and democratic society without free and democratic unions.

There are many who believe that moral values—or equity considerations—are incompatible with the requirements of economic efficiency: that people will only work out of a fear of starving, income support systems damage the economy, labor organizations and worker participation impair productivity, and measures to insure equal employment opportunity are incompatible with the efficiency requirements of a competitive free market economy. Equity measures can admittedly detract from economic efficiency, but I am convinced that in the long run viable, sustainable, efficient organizations are those which stress the dignity of work and appeal to higher nonmaterial values and justice.

The Meaning of Justice

Although justice can be undergirded by enlightened self-interest, its strong base is religion, which deals with such fundamental matters as basic human nature, the meaning and purpose of life, our relationship to each other and our creator. Of course, religion does not provide answers to specific problems at specific points in time. Specific answers are provided by politics, economics, and personal decisions. But religion provides a guide to these processes and should establish the framework within which personal decisions are made. Religious differences—especially in the Judaeo-Christian tradition—are much less important for ethical purposes than the large areas of common ground.

While there are natural moral laws, these must be interpreted in different historical contexts. This is especially important in periods of ferment like the 1970s and 1980s which appear to be a period of transition— from what some call the industrial to the postindustrial society. I do not like that terminology because it implies that ours is no longer an industrial society. If we are to remain a major world economic power, as I believe we must for moral as well as economic reasons, we will preserve and strengthen our basic industries. Indeed, the distinction between "smokestack" and "high tech" industries is a false dichotomy: If the smokestack industries make it, they will do so by using the most advanced information technology.

It seems to me that it is better to call ours an *internationalized information society*. The internationalization of the American economy has been one of the most significant developments since 1950. The proportion of GNP accounted for by international transactions has increased from 9 percent to 25 percent and almost three-fourths of American products are now subject to international competition. The internationalization of world financial, commodity, goods, and (to a lesser extent) labor markets has dramatically altered the viability conditions for American industries and workers. The efficiency requirements of international competition have put a much greater premium on productivity, quality output, and flexibility.

The Judaeo-Christian Concept of Justice

The Bible does not define the term, but the commandment to do justice occupied a central place in both the Old and New Testaments. Amos warned the worshippers at Bethel and Gilgal:

> "I hate, I despise your feasts, and I take no delight in your solemn assemblies. Even though you offer me your burnt offerings, I will not accept them, and the peace offerings of your fatted beasts I will not look upon. Take away from me the noise of your songs; to the melody of your harps I will not listen. But let justice roll down like the waters, and righteousness like an ever-flowing stream." (Amos, 5:21-24.)

The biblical conception of justice also is not the same as the legal principle of equal protection of the laws. The scriptures do not mandate *neutrality*, but a positive bias for the protection and restoration of the vulnerable, the poor, the oppressed. Justice is insisting that the vulnerable members of the community be included in the well-being of the community. Justice means standing with the lowliest neighbor, rejecting the worship of wealth and power, and creating structures supportive of all.

According to Jim Wallis in *The Call to Conversion*, "Jesus talks more about wealth and poverty than any other subject, including heaven and hell, sexual morality, the law, and violence." (Harper and Row, 1982, p. 58.) Jesus reminds us of the dangers of wealth and power. "You cannot serve God and mammon." (Luke 16:13.) "Take heed and beware of all covetousness, for life does not consist in the abundance of possessions." (Luke 12:15.) "How hard it is for those who have riches to enter the Kingdom of God."

Wealth does not exclude one from the Kingdom, but it does create dangers. The wealthy and powerful have special temptations to attribute both wealth and power exclusively to their personal merit, to oppress the less fortunate, and to blind themselves to their neighbors' needs.

The scriptures make it clear, moreover, that justice is a concern of government or civil authorities as well as individuals. According to John Calvin, the civil authorities are called and appointed to be God's deputies. The calling of civil authority is "not only holy and lawful before God, but also the most sacred and by far the most honorable of all callings in the whole life of mortal men." (*Institutes*, Bk. IV, Ch. 20, Sec. 4.) The officeholder is called to do justice, to administer the structures of justice, to be a protector and guardian of the laws, and to see to it that the various ends of government are achieved.

It is well-known that Calvin stressed frugality, honesty, and industry, but he also warned against the

dangers of prosperity, greed, and the tendency for the
wealthy and powerful to exploit others.

The corruptibility of government and the sus-
ceptibility of magistrates to the abuse of power require
laws and constitutional guarantees to preserve the
common good and prevent the government itself from
being dominated by any class or sector of society. The
government must concern itself with the victims of
greed and unjust gain as well as the victims of indifference and of systemic inequality and violence.

Calvin's concept of justice and injustice is closely
related to the rationale for a democratic society. As
Reinhold Neibuhr put it: "Man's capacity for justice
makes democracy possible, but man's inclination to
injustice makes democracy necessary."

Power

As noted, religion provides a general guide to conduct but does not necessarily furnish detailed answers
to specific problems. This is done by political and
economic processes. These relationships involve the
use of different kinds of power, which can be defined
as the ability to cause or to prevent change. Con-
ceptually, power may be defined as economic, physical, or moral, with political power as a conglomerate
type—i.e., the use of other forms by the State in
response to political pressures. Economic power is the
ability to cause or to prevent change by conveying or
withholding goods and services; moral power appeals
to fundamental concepts of rightness. Physical
power—the ultimate power of the State—is the ability

to cause or prevent change through the threat or use of physical force.

Rough checks and balances exist because of some apparent trade-offs in the use of different kinds of power. There seems to be an inverse relationship, for example, between economic and physical power on the one hand and moral power on the other. This can be called the "underdog" effect. Examples of this were the public support for unions in the 1930s, when organized labor's economic power was at its lowest. Conversely, as unions, business, or other groups acquire economic power they tend to lose moral support. Moral power also is related to how well a particular group performs its basic function in society. If, for example, business appears to be managing effectively, it gains moral as well as economic power. The same applies to unions—they gain moral power as they appear to be effectively advancing the common good rather than narrow special interests.

The reason moral power is so important in the long run is that parties not immediately involved in power contests tend to judge the contestants mainly on moral grounds, and, in the long run in an interdependent society, "disinterested" parties can support or damage a country, organization, group, etc. Thus, while economic and physical power often seem to be controlling in the short run, in a longer period these are less powerful than moral forces.

The Practical Implications

Moral considerations have very practical implications for nations, organizations, or individuals.

Indeed, individual rights relative to governments are related to a society's conception of the origin of personal rights. As the Declaration of Independence put it, we have certain unalienable rights which we derive from our creator—not from the government. The government's duty is to protect these rights. If the government becomes oppressive or "destructive of these ends," it is the right of the people to alter and abolish the government. This concept is the ultimate safeguard of a free society, which ordinarily can rely on the rule of law to protect liberty.

Moral concerns also have a strong bearing on our standing in the world community—especially among those people who share our values. Our unity, morale, and will to sustain and project our system are directly related to our faithfulness to moral principles.

Similarly, many of the world's problems are related to the proper relationships with other peoples, even those we regard as adversaries or potential adversaries. This does not, of course, require a naive approach to international affairs. We do not have to agree with the Soviets, for example, to communicate with them and to realize our mutual advantage in such matters as nuclear arms limitations. We should be eager to compete with the Soviets in terms of basic systems. We will be weaker if our competition with them causes us to develop their tactics or to ignore the need for frank and open cooperation on international issues.

We must be also particularly concerned about justice in Third World countries where unemployment and underemployment approach 50 percent; purely aside from moral concerns about the human condition, these Third World problems will visit us through immigration, political unrest, or international trade. Moreover, grave dangers are presented to world peace by growing extremes in wealth and income within these countries and between the rich and poor countries at a time when so much is being spent on arms. A broader view of our own self-interest requires that we be concerned about justice in these countries as well as our own. In other words, the community we must be concerned about is not just in the United States.

Moral imperatives also are involved in maximizing the advantages and minimizing the dangers of conflict in a heterogeneous country like ours. There is great strength and vitality in our cultural, racial, demographic, and geographic diversity. But there also is the lurking danger of social unrest and racial, ethnic, or religious conflict.

Unions and Income Distribution

Widening inequalities in wealth and income could exacerbate those social tensions. There is a growing concern among some analysts, for example, about the tendency for international trade, the growth of information technology and our wage determining processes to eliminate high wage jobs for blue-collar workers and to create a few high paying engineering, scientific, and technical jobs on the one hand and more low paying service jobs on the other. Wassily Leontief, Nobel laureate in economics, even raises the long-run problem of massive unemployment because of the rapid introduction of information technology. Leontief argues that the nineteenth-century industrial revolution greatly improved workers' welfare because the technology of that era made workers indispensable and improved their productivity. With rising productivity and collective bargaining, workers acquired the power both to improve their conditions and to participate in making the rules governing working conditions. The newer information technology, by contrast, can replace eyes, ears, and brains—not just brawn—and therefore makes labor more dispensable. The older technology not only improved productivity, but also concentrated workers in large, urban factories, making it possible for them to more easily form trade unions to protect themselves. The newer technology reverses all of these trends: It accelerates the decentralization of industry to rural areas and low wage areas in the United States and overseas; it facilitates the substitution of women for men, a process which apparently is widening the pay gap between men and women with the same human capital characteristics; it decentralizes labor into smaller work units and increases the proportion of managerial, professional, technical, and service workers; and, finally, the large oligopolistic goods-producing firm, where unions were concentrated, has been rendered obsolete by international competition and the new technology.

The main operating procedure for traditional American unions has been to remove labor from competition, a procedure they increasingly are unable to follow in the internationalized information society. In short, labor organizations are no longer able to protect their members through traditional collective bargaining processes alone. The logical answer would be for unions to organize internationally in order to form countervailing power to international corporations, but this is unlikely to happen in the immediate future: Workers remain very nationalistic, have very limited power to organize in the developing countries, and are not likely to risk their jobs in a job-short world. The mobility of scarce capital obviously gives the multinational employer a clear advantage over trade unions. American employers have generally been more hostile to trade unions than their counterparts in other democratic industrial countries, which surprises some foreigners, because ours is the only major labor movement to openly embrace capitalism. In the 1970s, American employers became more aggressively anti-union, forming a Council for a Union-Free Environment and stepping up the effort to eliminate trade unions from such strongholds as construction and transportation.

As a result of all of these trends, union membership has declined from about 35 percent of the nonagricultural labor force in the 1950s to less than 20 percent today. There are those who predict the obsolescence of unions in the internationalized information world.

The relative decline of unions raises important issues for a free society. Unions emerged with industralization to promote the interests of workers in a pluralistic society—in political as well as economic matters. It has been received doctrine, at least since the 1930s, that industrialized countries could not be

free and democratic unless they had free and democratic labor movements. Protection of the right to
organize and bargain collectively was defended during
the 1930s on both economic and equity grounds. Economically, unions helped raise workers' wages and
therefore helped sustain the purchasing power needed
to avoid recession. Moreover, by raising wages,
unions spurred management to higher productivity.

The framers of the National Labor Relations Act
likewise considered it equitable to make it possible for
workers to organize and bargain collectively. Before
the 1930s, the government had encouraged business
organizations, through corporate and other forms of
business organization, while using its power to prevent workers from organizing. Even without the government's help, most large employers had far more
bargaining power than individual employees. The
National Labor Relations Act was based in part on the
biblical conception of justice: Collective bargaining
was needed because it was unjust to treat unequals as
equals in contracting. Hence, it was considered more
just to permit workers to decide for themselves
whether or not they wanted to organize and bargain
collectively.

The right to decide for or against unions in
government-supervised elections was a unique—and
valuable—feature of the American industrial relations
system. In most other countries, class consciousness
caused workers to be much better organized politically
and economically than in the United States, making it
very difficult for employers to avoid dealing with
workers' organizations. The American workers' right

to vote in representative elections introduced an element of flexibility not present in other systems. The competition between union and nonunion sectors of various industries caused more price flexibility, and the competition between unions and employers caused both to be more concerned about promoting workers' interests. There is little question, for example, that nonunion employers treat their workers better because of the threat of unionization. Nor is there much doubt that the right of workers to vote for or against unions in representation elections was an important factor overcoming racial discrimination by labor organizations and making them more responsive to the concerns of women.

The role of labor organizations in giving workers a voice in political and economic affairs is sufficiently important to warrant serious concern about the antiunion attitudes of American employers. At the philosophical level, most employers realize that we cannot have a free and democratic society without a free and democratic labor movement. At the personal and political level, on the other hand, employers would like to operate without the need to bargain with unions. However, the employers' choice is not whether the United States has a labor movement, but what kind. Experience suggests that workers tend to form moderate, cooperative labor unions if those organizations have the ability to protect and promote workers' interests. Otherwise, labor organizations become both more political and less supportive of the existing system.

From the public perspective, therefore, both the

interests of workers and the needs of a free society can best be enhanced by strengthening the workers' freedom of choice with respect to collective bargaining and freedom of association in the political process. It is not in the national interest for this choice to be weakened by ineffective and lengthy administrative processes which dilute and delay the workers' freedom of choice, as has happened in recent years. Moreover, the weak penalties for violation of the National Labor Relations Act make it possible for some employers to decide that it is cheaper to disobey the law. Fortunately, the public's moral condemnation of this practice causes employers to change their behavior in the long run, but workers' rights are damaged in the short run.

Cooperation and Worker Participation

Another movement affecting workers in a free society has been the emergence of various forms of worker participation in the industrialized democracies. Worker participation takes many forms and is supported by a wide variety of motives. Although it is not at all clear where these processes are going in the United States and other countries, several broad patterns are emerging. In the United States, worker involvement in decisionmaking has been supported mainly by employers who believe that worker participation at the shop-floor level has been a major factor in the competitiveness of their rivals in other countries, especially Japan and the "little Japans" emerging in the Pacific Basin. Worker participation and job security through "lifetime employment" are components of a Japanese system that has been incredibly competitive. The Japanese model stresses quality output, productivity, and flexibility through worker involvement and job security for the basic core of the work force. Flexibility is achieved through a variety of choices, including: a worker compensation system that provides as much as one-third of the workers' annual income depending on company performance; the use of subcontracting; production sharing whereby low wage work on components of a product is allocated to other countries while the higher valued activity is retained in Japan; and the use of secondary labor forces and other buffers to absorb shocks caused by changes in demand or external economic forces. While the Japanese system is very competitive, it has some features that would make it unacceptable in the United States. Women, for example, rarely have "lifetime" employment and are part of the buffer; this practice would be illegal in the United States. Moreover, only about 15 to 20 percent of the Japanese work force is part of the stable core with job security, although it can be argued that the flexibility provided by the "shock absorbers" gives the whole system greater stability.

This basic Japanese system is supported by other procedures that give Japanese firms competitive advantages. Japanese companies are likely to be able to take a longer time perspective than their American counterparts because of their equity financing sources. The Japanese rely much more on the banks, whose backing by the government can minimize risks. Moreover, Japanese banks are allowed to make equity investments in companies (a practice prohibited by

the Glass-Steagal Act in the United States). The
Japanese companies' stockholders are therefore more
likely to be other companies whose businesses are
closely related. The American companies' heavy reliance on the stock market causes an excessive preoccupation with short-run quarterly earnings
statements—a process former GE chairman Reg Jones
called the "tyranny of Wall Street." This short-run
perspective also causes many American companies to
ignore the technological requirements for international competitiveness.

The basic motives of large American and Japanese
companies also are likely to be different. The American company is more likely to stress profit maximization and stockholders' rights while the Japanese company is more likely to stress increasing market shares
and concern for its permanent work force. The emphasis on stockholders' rights in many American companies is really a subterfuge for control by company
executives who often vote themselves very high salaries and bonuses regardless of company performance.
The incomes of American executives relative to workers are likely to be much larger than their Japanese
counterparts. American managements are able to control their companies because the diffusion of large
numbers of stockholders makes it possible for many
large public corporations to be controlled with no
more than 15 percent of the stock. While these management practices are legal, they raise serious equity
issues. Indeed, some management specialists have
termed these practices "legalized embezzlement."
(Peter Drucker, *Managing in Turbulent Times*, New

York: Harper and Row, 1982.) The long-run viability of corporations in a free society is threatened by management practices that are condemned by the public. These practices also exacerbate labor-management relations, which already are much more adversarial than those in other countries with more competitive enterprises.

It would, however, be a mistake to assume that the superior performance of the Japanese economy is due entirely or even mainly to Japanese management. The Japanese are much more unified as a nation because of their defeat in World War II and the fact that their limited physical resources have forced them to make much better investments in their people and to develop more productive and flexible institutions.

The Japanese are much better at national consensus building than we are in the United States, which probably is more responsible for their superior economic performance than their management practices. The Japanese system rests on respect for the dignity and opinions of individuals. It is assumed, for example, that workers have important contributions to make to the production process and to national economic policymaking. It also is assumed that worker dedication and commitment to the enterprise is essential to quality, productivity, and flexibility. Authoritarian American management systems are based on the assumptions that there is one "best" way to do things, that management knows that best way, and that its job is to impose that system on the workers. This authoritarian system with its lack of respect for the worker's opinion and dignity creates a less productive, more legalistic and adversarial process that is incompatible with both the quality and productivity requirements of a free and democratic society. It is, for example, difficult for workers to make the transition from being responsible adults in a democratic society outside the firm to a restricted childlike dependency on the job.

As noted, however, more and more American companies recognize the obsolescence of the traditional oligopolistic and authoritarian models and are attempting to become more competitive by introducing quality control circles, quality of work life, and other forms of worker participation in order to make themselves more competitive. Moreover, worker representatives are now serving on the boards of directors of a growing number of major American corporations.

It is too early to tell whether these forms of worker involvement are "passing fads" or a permanent movement, but I would bet on the latter. The better educated American work force and the efficiency requirements of the internationalized information economy require greater worker involvement. Quality is a very important requirement for competitiveness in the new environment, and it is very difficult to compel quality. Moreover, more companies will undoubtedly learn what our best ones already know: that in the long run the highest profits are not made by those who concentrate on profit maximization but by those who appeal to superordinate values inside the firm and out. It is hard to motivate people to excellence for material gain alone. Much greater satisfaction is likely to come from innovation and quality output based on concepts of service, stewardship, and fair treatment of workers and the public.

Peters and Waterman in their popular book, *In Search of Excellence*, conclude that one of the attributes characterizing excellent American companies was that they were "value driven." William Ouichi in his book *Theory Z* concludes:

> "The bedrock of any successful company is its philosphy. The thought of mixing practical business matters with pie in the sky concerns may seem strange, but popular beliefs aside, philosophy and business are the most compatible bedfellows." (p. 111.)

This concept also guided Tom Watson of IBM, one of America's most successful companies. As a *Fortune* writer expressed it:

> "Whether you particularly agree with [what Mr. Watson is saying] you listen . . . Let him discourse on the manifest destiny of IBM and you are ready to join the company for life. Let him detail plain homilies of the values of vision, and a complex and terrifying world becomes transparent and simple. Let him explain the necessity of giving religion preference over everything else, and you could not help falling to your knees. . . . Everybody in the organization is expected to find [IBM's] ubiquitous THINK sign a constant source of inspiration, as the weary travelers of old found new strength in wayside crucifixes." (Gil Burck, "IBM," *Fortune*, January 1940, pp. 36-40.)

It is likewise highly probable that the international information society will cause other transformations. Large public corporations either will develop codes of conduct for their management or probably will be subjected to public regulation. Either they will voluntarily become stewards, conservers, and developers of resources in a sustaining environment, or efforts will be made to force them to do so by law. The large multinational corporation will become more concerned about the welfare of its workers and the communities in which they live or those corporations will lose public support. In other words, companies must pay attention to their moral power or they will lose some of their freedom.

The international information society also could raise serious problems for workers if, as Wassily Leontief suggests, evolving technology makes workers dispensable, making it very difficult to provide good jobs to all who want them. It is clear that whatever its ultimate net effects, technology will displace many workers, requiring adjustment processes through work flexibility, education, and training.

A shortage of good jobs would create other problems for workers. There could be a growing polarization of income distribution between the unemployed and low wage workers on one side and the growing few who receive large incomes from the ownership of property and the possession of good jobs on the other. However, the implications of polarizing income distributions in a democratic society suggest probable measures to halt the process. One would be the use of political power by the "have nots" (based in part by moral appeals to the public) to transfer income to them from the "haves." A better solution would be to widen the income base to make it possible for workers to supplement wages through income from equity ownership in companies and bonuses depending on company performance. The polarization of the distribution of income also could be counteracted by the apparent trend toward greater entrepreneurship and smaller producing units, which would reintroduce the upward mobility within the smaller producing units of the preindustrial society, especially if workers have greater access to education, training, and physical capital. It is interesting to note that the recent contract by the United Auto Workers and General Motors establishes a fund to provide venture capital to GM employees who wish to go into business for themselves. The incomes of American farmers improved with mechanization because farmers owned the technology and land as well as supplied the labor. Providing wider ownership to American workers would not only give them a greater stake in the success of their enterprise but also might make it possible for them to accumulate wealth as well.

The Future of Unions

There are those who think that labor organizations have become either irrelevant or obsolete in the internationalized information world. I do not share this belief. As long as there are workers there will be a need for organizations to protect their interests. However, it is reasonably certain that labor organizations will change their forms and procedures. American unions historically have been mainly male blue-collar organizations concentrated in large oligopolistic goods-producing organizations, or they have been organizations of highly skilled workers. The decline in union membership is due to the fact that the work force is shifting more to smaller, nonurban, and female work forces. Moreover, the internationalization of the American economy makes it difficult for unions to follow their traditional policies of removing labor from competition through wage equalization and pattern bargaining.

Unions also suffer from the fact that the macro-economic policies that were compatible with their traditional bargaining procedures are less effective in an internationalized information world. Keynesian demand management policies were designed primarily for relatively closed domestic economies. These policies contained an inflationary bias and are less effective in the internationalized environment because efforts to stimulate the American economy will simply stimulate imports if other economies are not expanding at the same pace. The alternative to demand management, monetarism, tends to translate wage increases above productivity changes into unemployment. Efforts to maintain wages above levels compatible with international competition in this environment will lead to sustained high levels of unemployment. Moreover, while collective bargaining has not been an initiating source of inflation in recent years, many industrial relations practices tend to accelerate those pressures—these include competitive pattern bargaining and cost of living adjustments.

The viability conditions for organized labor are similar to those of business enterprises. They must be more concerned with flexibility and productivity. More flexible compensation systems could serve as shock absorbers to changes in demand and could increase worker commitment to improved productivity. The challenge for labor organizations is to supplement their traditional concern for sharing the economic gains of an enterprise with greater attention to increasing those gains and maintaining the competitiveness of the enterprises. Unions also must change work practices that prevent improvements in productivity, and management must be more concerned about worker security as well as genuine worker participation. Companies like IBM with "full employment" strategies have found that greater security for employees improves their performance and strengthens management.

Unions, like companies, must be concerned about their moral imperatives. Like other organizations, unions are not likely to be revitalized if they ignore superordinate or higher values. Indeed, the periods of greatest vitality for American unions have come when they have been regarded as "causes" or organizations to improve the common good and not just another business or special interest. To a greater degree than most other institutions, unions have in fact championed causes that helped all workers and indeed all citizens. But unions have not done a very good job of projecting a positive image. In part this is because corruption in some unions has been widely publicized. Moreover, because they have been placed in a position of trying to protect their members' jobs and

wages, unions appear to be resisting inevitable
changes needed to make the American economy more
productive. Unions are not likely to act "responsibly,"
however, unless their members' legitimate concerns
are met and the unions are accepted as full partners in
national decisionmaking processes.

National Policies

Free institutions also are not likely to be competitive without appropriate national economic policies.
Indeed, I am convinced that the greatest obstacle to
the full realization of our national potential has more to
do with inadequate public policies than to deficiencies
in our private institutions. And the country's increasing divisiveness and adversarial processes are major
obstacles to sound policies based on consensus. A
number of factors divide Americans: our relative safety
from external threats, our heterogeneous population,
our relative affluence, and the individualistic heritage
relating to our origins as a nation. Our major challenge
is to retain the dynamic advantages of individualism
and cultural diversity while recognizing our community of interest and the need for social justice for those
who are most vulnerable.

It is unfortunately true that the last unifying experience the United States had was World War II. But war
will no longer be a source of national unity. The only
unifying war is likely to be an all-out conflict like
World War II, which is unthinkable in a nuclear age;
all other conflicts are likely to be partial and divisive
wars like those in Viet Nam and Central America. It is
unfortunate, moreover, that people seem to require

wars to become unified. What we need to find, in William James' terms, is the "moral equivalent of war" in promoting peace and tackling some of our difficult national and international problems. Perhaps a youth service corps would help unite young people from different racial, ethnic, and social backgrounds. The service corps could perform much useful work in the United States and other countries that would do infinitely more good for national security than the nuclear arms race. The attachment of GI Bill-type educational benefits to such a corps would help prevent polarizing people according to educational levels.

Reducing conflict also requires some attitudinal changes. A moral imperative is that we not stereotype other people and make abstractions of human suffering. For example, unemployed people face considerable stress and often blame themselves for their unemployment. Public attitudes which blame the unemployed for their unemployment are not only unfair, but exacerbate their stress problems.

Many of our income support programs are seriously flawed and need major reforms—this is especially true of the welfare system. But myths about those on welfare not wanting to work and attitudes which assume that welfare and disability recipients are probably cheats make matters worse. Instead of viewing these programs as the way we provide justice to the vulnerable in a modern industrialized society and as investment in our people, we too often view them as "necessary evils" and make that a self-fulfilling prophecy.

We also must guard against attitudes based on an exaggerated sense of self worth. Many people get wealthy because they render services to the community—they create wealth; others, because they inherited it or were lucky. However we get our wealth, we have to be pretty arrogant to think that it is entirely because of our own merit and that we owe nothing to our community and country. This attitude concerning wealth was one reason for the biblical warning about the spiritual damage of wealth and power to the wealthy and powerful themselves. Individualism has great social value, but individualism run amok can cause great social damage.

One of our greatest needs is to develop mechanisms to build bipartisan consensus for important national interests—such as basic economic, social, foreign, and national security policies. As a nation, a community, we have much greater common interests in these policies than differences. Consensus mechanisms based on mutual respect and a desire to gain agreement on the facts can do a lot, both to reduce functionless conflict and to provide better information to all sectors of our society. Continuing discussions also improve understanding. A prerequisite to these mechanisms is adequate representation by people affected by the policy, which requires mutual acceptance of the legitimacy of the different actors. For example, a national economic policy mechanism should include representatives of the public and private sectors—labor, business, consumers, finance, and others as appropriate with government officials representing the public interest. These mechanisms could do much to improve public education and understanding.

Every country with superior economic performance on many change indicators has some way to build consensus except the United States. I believe the absence of such a mechanism is one of our main disadvantages relative to other countries and a major reason it is so hard for us to protect the public interest from narrow special interests. Moreover, the absence of consensus makes it difficult to develop policies to make the best use of our resources and realize our national potential. Most of our economic policy problems are more *political* than economic; partisan politics makes it difficult for economic policymakers to follow steady policies to achieve stable growth and full employment.

One reason for resistance to such mechanisms is the unwillingness of some groups to accept others,— especially for business groups to accept organized labor—or most well-organized groups to give up their special interest advantage or to recognize the legitimacy of other groups. There also is a fear that such mechanisms will recommend greater government involvement in the economy. Negativism about government has some basis in fact, and we should avoid excessive government involvement in private affairs; but the common idea that government produces nothing of value, while popular this day, is clearly absurd. Indeed, most of America's international success stories have been where there have been active public-private partnerships—agriculture, information technology, aircraft, etc. Unfortunately, powerful economic interests also adopt laissez-faire attitudes because they know truly democratic government involvement would protect vulnerable members of society and the public interest from them.

Conclusion

Some economists see a dichotomy between equity and efficiency, but in the long run moral concerns are likely to enhance efficiency more than they damage it—especially if we count social as well as individual and budget costs. Companies, unions, nations, and individuals that are motivated by "superordinate values" are more likely to achieve excellence (happiness, satisfaction) than those motivated mainly by narrow material gain. Public policies based on a genuine concern for the vulnerable not only preserve a vision of a just and humane society but help build unity and facilitate the conservation and development of our resources. An internationalized information world puts a premium on productivity, quality, and flexibility, all of which require much greater consensus building and participation.

Consensus requires adequate representation of major actors. A major problem in the United States is inadequate participation by workers. We are not likely to have a free and democratic society unless workers have the freedom to decide for themselves whether or not they want to bargain collectively and be represented by labor organizations on the job and in public processes. It is therefore important to preserve that right. However, unions as well as companies need to adjust their policies and procedures to the realities of an internationalized information world.

Finally, we must recognize the value to us of carrying out our moral responsibilities in a dangerous, uncertain, and increasingly interdependent world. Freedom is indivisible. We cannot have freedom, prosperity, and security unless all major groups share in that prosperity—a reality that applies to the world as well as to groups within a country.

MORALITY AND PRAGMATISM
IN FOREIGN POLICY

by

Eugene V. Rostow

Eugene V. Rostow

Professor Rostow was educated at Yale University and King's College, Cambridge. He joined the faculty of the Yale Law School in 1938 and was named Sterling Professor of Law and Public Affairs in 1964. He is presently Sterling Professor of Law Emeritus and Senior Research Scholar, Yale University, and Distinguished Visiting Research Professor of Law and Diplomacy, National Defense University.

Professor Rostow's record of public service is a distinguished one. During World War II he served as an advisor to the Department of State and later was assistant executive secretary of the Economic Commission for Europe of the United Nations. He was a part of both the Kennedy and Johnson administrations and was Undersecretary of State for Political Affairs from 1966 to 1969. He became Chairman of the Executive Committee of the Committee on the Present Danger in 1976. He was director of the Arms Control and Disarmament Agency from 1981 to 1983.

A fellow of the American Academy of the Arts and Sciences and a member of the American Law Institute, Professor Rostow has been decorated as a chevalier of the Legion d'Honneur and received honorary doctorates from several American universities. He has been George Eastman Visiting Professor and Fellow of Balliol College at Oxford University and has spoken in distinguished lecturer series throughout the United States.

Professor Rostow's books include Planning for Freedom *(1959),* The Sovereign Prerogative *(1962),* Law, Power, and the Pursuit of Peace *(1968),* Peace in the Balance *(1972), and* The Ideal in Law *(1978).*

MORALITY AND PRAGMATISM
IN FOREIGN POLICY

by

Eugene V. Rostow*

It is an honor to participate in this distinguished lecture series, and a challenge to address its theme.

My thesis is simple but neither easy nor popular. It is that in the years ahead both our most earthy, pragmatic, and fundamental security interests as a nation and the moral imperatives of our culture demand that the goal of our foreign policy be the pursuit of a nearly universal regime of international peace. It is commonplace to suppose that morality and what is often called "Realpolitik" or "power politics" represent opposing principles for the conduct of foreign relations. The circumstances of modern life require morality and Realpolitik to join hands. The paradox is not so shocking as it may appear. This is by no means the first time that democratic ideals have been reinforced by reality.

In a free and democratic society, it is hardly necessary to point out that international peace is a moral idea. Throughout history a few romantic souls have loved war and praised it as ennobling, or preached holy war in the service of political or religious crusades. But free societies are committed to the convic-

*The views expressed in this lecture are those of Professor Rostow, and not necessarily those of the National Defense University or the Department of Defense.

tion that peace among the states is good in itself, and the best possible environment for encouraging the achievement of other moral goals in social life. Under our moral code, this axiom fully justifies the profession of arms as we know it in the West.

In identifying international peace as one of the moral ideals of free societies, one should distinguish "peace" from what are loosely called "human rights." Of course the United States and other civilized societies should always encourage the universal acceptance and legal protection of human liberty. In the nature of things, they must; they do; and they will, unless they are cowed into a posture of ignoble silence on the subject by their fear of offending the leadership of the Soviet Union. But international peace is something quite different from antipathy to barbarism. To recall the language of the United Nations Charter, peace can be defined only as an effectively enforced rule of respect for the territorial integrity and political independence of all states, large and small, socialist or capitalist. In a world of states based on diverse social and political systems, the rule of peace is essential to the possibility of their peaceful coexistence.

If one examines the problem of our national security in the chilly perspective of power politics, one must reach the same conclusion. The United States and the other free societies have no alternative if they wish to survive: they must work together to achieve a general condition of peace throughout the world by seeing to it the rules against aggression necessary to the peaceful cooperation of states are generally and reciprocally obeyed. The free world has more than enough power and potential power to achieve that end. But the free people will summon up the will to do so only when they are convinced it is their inescapable duty.

A policy of neutrality and isolation from entangling alliances served the United States reasonably well during the century between 1815 and 1917, when a state of worldwide peace was maintained by the diplomatic Concert of Europe—not perfect peace by any means, but relative peace, and a great deal more peace than we have today. The memory of that period strongly appeals to the American mind. But isolationism and neutrality are no longer a feasible model for American foreign policy. Europe has lost the power to direct the orchestra. If the orchestra is to be led, we have to lead it. No other free state or combination of free states is capable of carrying out the task. World Wars I and II and their consequences; the dissolution of the old empires, except that of the Czars; the emergence of the Soviet Union, Japan, and China as major actors in world politics; and the adhesion of Germany and Japan to the Western Alliance system have transformed the dynamics of world power. At the same time, technological change—including the development of nuclear weapons and the position of the United States and the Soviet Union as nuclear superpowers—has revolutionized the art of war and made the world smaller, more volatile, more interdependent, more bipolar, and infinitely more dangerous. Because of the state of the nuclear balance, the United States cannot escape from the task of leading the quest for peace. No other country can provide a deterrent counterweight to Soviet nuclear power.

As a result, considerations of self-preservation now compel the United States to adapt, reform, and carry

out the foreign policy of coalition diplomacy through
which it has sought for nearly forty years to contain the
expansion of the Soviet Union. We cannot remind
ourselves too often that wise diplomacy in the style of
Churchill could have stopped Germany's drive for
hegemony and prevented both World Wars I and II.
Confronting the Soviet Union's bid for dominion in a
nuclear setting, the United States and its allies must
not repeat the mistakes of the weak and dilatory Western leaders before 1914 and 1939. Their goal now can
be nothing short of genuine peace. World Wars I and
II did unspeakable damage to the fabric of civilization.
The potentialities of nuclear war are manifestly worse.

Peace, whether domestic or international, is a complex idea. It involves much more than the absence of
violence. It posits a relationship of tranquillity among
people and states such that no person and no state
need fear its neighbors. Peace is a condition of organized society—of a society organized under a humane
and effective system of law. Law can never be enforced without some invocation of force at the mar-
gins. But law cannot be imposed by force alone. It
arises from the consent of the governed, not from the
barrel of a gun. Law implies a social order, but law is
much more than order. There can be order in tyrannical societies. The streets of the Soviet Union are
quiet, and there is no open warfare between the
Soviet Union and the states of Central Europe and—
except for Afghanistan—the states of Central Asia. But
there is no peace within the Soviet Union, and no
peace between the Soviet Union and its satellites and
other neighbors. The notion of peace—the notion,

that is, of the rule of law—denotes a society governed by a code of law derived from the customs and shared morality of the society and its culture, a law constantly growing in response to experience and to the changing moral aspirations of the people it purports to govern.

Is the diverse and turbulent community of states in the world a "society" and a "culture" in the sense in which I have been using these words—a system of states bound together by an accepted and effectively enforced corpus of international law—or is it no more than a wilderness through which the wary pilgrim must progress fully armed, always prepared for the worst, and alert to danger from every quarter? Is the code of law to which the international state system is nominally committed, the Charter of the United Nations, "law" in any meaningful sense or simply a collection of philosophers' dreams?

I shall start my answer to these questions with the distinction between "ideas" and "beliefs" made by the Spanish philosopher Ortega y Gasset:

"Beliefs are all those things that we absolutely take for granted even though we don't think about them. We are so certain they exist and that they are just as we take them to be, that we never question them, but instead take them automatically into account in our behavior. When we go down the street we never try to walk through the walls of buildings; we automatically avoid bumping into them without even having to think: 'Walls are impenetrable.' But there are also things and situations regarding which we find ourselves

without a firm belief: we sometimes wonder
whether certain things exist or not, whether they
are one way or another. When this happens we
have no alternative but to formulate an idea, an
opinion regarding them. Ideas, then, are those
'things' we consciously construct or elaborate because we *do not believe* in them. [Emphasis in
original.]"

Thus beliefs are part of the realm of intuition, and
ideas are tools of thought—the tentative hypotheses
we advance, test, and discard, one after another, as we
try to think rationally about our experience.

In Ortega's terms, most people "believe" that there
is a viable state system which functions effectively
throughout the world in accordance with an accepted
code of international law. This is necessarily the un-
stated premise behind proposals and resolutions one
hears and reads about nearly every day suggesting that
the United States withdraw its troops from Europe
and Asia, call the Navy back to home ports, and return
to the halcyon days of isolation and neutrality. After
all, we can telephone to London or Tokyo, ski in
Switzerland, and send letters or cargoes to Australia or
even to Beijing. Planes and ships crisscross the earth,
satellites fly above it, their paths organized by international agreement and often regulated by international agencies or national agencies cooperating
with great precision. We are accustomed to assume
that the pattern of international organization we see
and sense around us is immutable, and that it will
continue to exist without regard to the behavior of the
United States.

But the nearly universal belief in the continuity of the state system is an error. In its political structure, international society is as fragile as a stage set. This century has witnessed the breakup of ancient empires and the disappearance of dynasties more than a thousand years old. Once we liberate our minds from the illusion of the superobvious, it does not require much imagination to contemplate the circumstances under which the state system of our intuitive beliefs could be brought under Soviet control, and the evidence supporting the view that it is the goal of Soviet foreign policy to achieve that end. No doubt international arrangements for the control of the mail, aviation, and telecommunications would survive under a Pax Sovietica. But the state system would no longer be an association of the free and independent sovereignties which it is the goal of our policy to preserve.

The state system within which the United States and other free societies exist has evolved like other human institutions and has ebbed and flowed many times since the fall of Rome. When we can bring ourselves to think about the state system at all, two visions jostle for dominance in our minds: the vision of the jungle, on the one hand, with the nations in a Hobbesian state of nature where clubs are trumps; and, on the other, a vision of Utopian harmony where the relations among the nations are governed by pious respect for the rules of international law. Reality encompasses both elements in different combinations over time—the element of order and that of anarchy. Sometimes one factor is in the ascendant, sometimes the other. Modern history is a counterpoint to these two themes, a persistent but not a sustained nor a uniformly successful effort to impose the rule of law on the nations, especially with regard to the international use of force. There can be no question as to which of these themes is in the ascendant today.

The modern state system emerged from the moral and intellectual climate of the Enlightenment and from the experience with war of the preceding two centuries. Its dominant idea is that the strongest states have a special responsibility for keeping the peace by preventing, confining, and limiting the practice of international war. The Congress of Vienna in 1815 and the diplomacy of the Victorian age proved to be both creative and important in shaping the modern state system and establishing its basic rules.

After Napoleon was defeated at Waterloo, the state system began to take on its contemporary form. It was a balance of power system, maintained for a century by the cooperation and restraint of the European Great Powers. But the methods initiated by the Congress of Vienna failed tragically in 1914. The men who met at Versailles in 1919 tried to recreate the Vienna system through the League of Nations, but their effort lacked conviction, and the League collapsed within a few years.

After World War II, the yearning for peace expressed itself again, this time in San Francisco through the conference which adopted the United Nations Charter. In 1945, Western opinion was convinced that if only the great powers had enforced the rules of the League Covenant against aggression in Manchuria, Ethiopia, Spain, and Rhineland, World War II would never have taken place.

Article 2(4) of the United Nations Charter categorically condems the international use of force—"force," it should be noted, not "armed force" alone—against the territorial integrity or political independence of a state, except where justified by the inherent and historic right of individual or collective self-defense, which is not qualified in any way by the Charter. Enforcement of these rules is the chief function of the Security Council, which, on paper at least, has far more authority than any institution of the League. Its nominal power recalls that which Palmerston, Disraeli, and Bismarck exercised in fact during some of the diplomatic Congresses of the nineteenth century: the power to guide, direct, limit, cajole, conciliate, and, if necessary, to command and dispose of controversies which threaten the peace.

It would have been difficult to fulfill the hopes of the Charter even if the great powers had remained together after 1945. The old state system, after all, had tenacious habits of aggressive warfare, and the end of West European imperialism has given those habits new opportunities. But the Soviet Union withdrew from the alliance which won World War II once victory was assured, and since then moments of consensus among the Great Powers have been rare. Between the late 1940s and the 1970s, the Western nations helped to enforce the rules of minimal world public order prescribed by the Charter quite effectively in their effort to contain Soviet expansion, but it has been obvious for the last fifteen years that the Charter of the United Nations is going the way of the Covenant of the League of Nations as an influence on the state system. At the moment, as the Secretary General of

the United Nations warned in his 1983 Annual Report,
the great danger facing the world is anarchy itself—a
condition of affairs which has always led to war.

The root of the matter is that the Soviet Union has
never accepted Article 2(4) of the United Nations
Charter as applicable to it. From the beginning of the
Charter era, the Soviet Union has claimed for itself—
and only for itself—the privilege of using force against
the territorial integrity or political independence of
states which are not governed by socialist regimes,
and indeed of using force even against socialist states if
they are under the control of socialist heretics, revisionists, or schismatics, or if they show dangerous
signs of backsliding to capitalism or democracy. One of
the most familiar Soviet tactics of aggression is the
international use of force in support of insurrections
within a state—a violation of state sovereignty which
international law has condemned as war for centuries.

This feature of the political landscape since 1945 is
so familiar to us that we take it to be the order of
nature and assume that it has somehow been legitimized. But the special privilege of the Soviet Union to
commit aggression at will cannot be legitimized under
the Charter of the United Nations. Whether practiced
by the Soviet Union or by any other state,
aggression—including the international use of force to
support revolutionary movements—breaches the basic rule of the Charter system: the integrity of states.

When pressed, Soviet diplomats or scholars say that
for the Motherland of Socialism to obey Article 2(4)
would be to give up its nature as a society and a state.
To this, the only answer an American can offer is that
the Soviet Union can preach the gospel of communism

as much as it likes, but that in the nature of the state system, it cannot be allowed to propagate its faith with a sword.

The Soviet program of expansion, sedulously pursued since 1945, has gone too far. It threatens the most fundamental security interest of all other states—their interest in the world balance of power—and has, therefore, touched nerves of great sensitivity in countries as diverse as China, Japan, and Egypt, in the NATO countries, and in the nations of Southeast Asia. Unless the policy of Soviet expansion is stopped—and stopped soon—it will destroy the last vestiges of the rule against aggression the world has struggled so hard and so long to establish. The state system cannot live by a double standard. Nations do not stand idly by and allow themselves to be nibbled to death, as Adlai Stevenson remarked a generation ago. This is not a result the Western nations want. Indeed, it is a result they profoundly fear. But it will come about, inevitably, if the Soviet Union continues on its present course.

Recognizing this state of affairs, the United States, its allies in NATO Europe, Japan, and other Western countries have soberly and reluctantly begun to restore the military balance between the Soviet Union and the West. This giant step, indispensable as it is, is only half the job. The United States has not yet put forward a coherent vision of Western foreign policy—a vision to which our people and those of our allies and other friendly nations could rally.

The reason for our silence on that subject is not obscure: It is Vietnam. We have not seriously begun to recover from the shock of the Vietnam experience

in defining the ends and means of our foreign policy;
politicians and others are afraid of reviving the passions of the Vietnam period.

One can distinguish a number of positions beneath
the surface of the American and Western debate about
the future of American foreign policy.

An increasingly influential body of American opinion implicitly or explicitly supports the view that, in a
nuclear world, it should be the policy of the United
States to defend only "Fortress America." Voices from
every part of the American political spectrum tell us
that the state of nuclear balance requires us to accept
such a posture and the political impotence it implies.
This would be a fatal mistake; our foreign policy since
the time of President Truman has not been dominated
by altruism but by the hard necessity of achieving and
maintaining a worldwide balance of power. The revi-
val of American isolationism would abandon that task.

Others suggest that we ignore the Third World, so
turbulent and unsettled in the aftermath of Empire,
and confine our security horizon to the NATO allies.
This line of policy would also be suicidal for the United
States and the other Western industrial democracies.
The world is round, and the industrial democracies
can be enveloped and neutralized from the Third
World. And the Third World is full of raw materials,
developing industries, and strategic choke points of
great importance to sea and air transportation. The
Third World matters a great deal. Both World Wars I
and II were triggered by conflicts which began in the
Third World. So did the innumerable wars which have
occurred since 1945. Even if we exclude the moral
factor from our foreign policies completely, there is no

way for the industrial democracies to wash their hands of the Third World and leave it sink into a morass of anarchy, famine, and Soviet domination.

Others believe we could survive by defending the NATO allies and Japan and our interests in the Middle East, or other areas which become critical to the balance of power in the context of Soviet campaigns of expansion. While this position comes closer to reality than proposals for a return to isolationism, a NATO-only policy, or a policy of ignoring the Third World, it too is fatally flawed. There are no parts of the Third World which could not become significant elements in the Soviet policy of expansion. Angola, South Yemen, and Afghanistan seem unbelievably remote from the United States. Yet they are all fronts in the worldwide struggle.

Finally, we must ask ourselves whether the national security interests of the United States in a nuclear world can be defended only by pressing for a policy of defense against all or nearly all aggression and organizing regional coalitions to fulfill that principle.

Until these questions are clearly and firmly answered, there will be no general consensus in the West on what our armed forces are for, or on when and how they should be used. Consequently, the influence of our armed forces in deterring aggression will be uncertain.

Those pressing questions constitute the next great task of American leadership. How should they be answered? What *are* the vital security interests of the United States, the interests for which we should fight if necessary, in a world which has been transformed by revolutions in politics, technology, and demography?

It is a truism of history that the most fundamental national security interest of every nation committed to peace is the balance of power. The phrase embodies the oldest and most familiar idea in the lexicon of thought about international affairs, indeed, of thought about social organization more generally. The Constitution of the United States and many of our laws apply the balance of power principle directly to the problem of preventing any one center of government, any part of the country, or any social class from accumulating enough power to dominate society. This is what the separation of powers, federalism, the antitrust laws, and the decentralized structure of our banking system are about. The problems of achieving a stable equilibrium between order and freedom in international society are the same as those which faced the men who established and then developed our national and federal union. Thus Thucydides wrote that the true cause of the Pelopennesian War was not one or another of the episodes of friction which occurred between Greek cities, but the rise in the power of Athens and the fear this caused in Sparta. And when Napoleon invaded Russia, even Jefferson, who had been a devout supporter of France and the French Revolution, became alarmed. If France, already the master of Western Europe, conquered Russia, Jefferson commented, it would have so much power that it could readily spare some to send against us in America.

The consciousness of the balance of power as the ultimate foundation of peace is universal, often giving rise to strong and even violent reactions almost as conditioned reflexes. Under such pressures, people and nations react in patterns they can rarely explain. But those patterns nonetheless are rational and predictable. Thus for centuries Britain sent troops to fight on the continent in order to keep Spain, France, or Germany from dominating Europe; for the same reason, the United States entered World War I in 1917, although most Americans thought we were fighting to protect the freedom of the seas and to make the world safe for democracy. Similarly, Britain and France fought the Crimean War to keep Russia out of the Middle East and the Mediterranean—a policy, incidentally, which worked for about a century. The younger Pitt tried repeatedly to appease revolutionary France and remain neutral in the war on the continent of Europe. He realized that his effort was hopeless only when France attacked Holland and the mouth of the Scheldt, thus engaging in aggression against one of Britain's ultimate security interests, which was also protected by treaty.

But the idea of the balance of power is no more than a starting point in analyzing the national security interests of the United States. In considering the security of the United States or any other particular country, the first question to face is what geographical areas are relevant. Obviously, the question would be answered differently in the age of sailing ships and in that of ballistic missiles, nuclear weapons, airplanes, and submarines. Thucydides wrote about the security of Athens and Sparta in a corner of the Mediterranean; Persia and the barbarians of the north were the most distant factors in his calculations, and the weapons affecting his analysis were swords, javelins, and ships propelled mainly by oars. The problems of Caesar and

Alexander were regional, and so were those of Europe, China, and Japan until the explorers and adventurers of the last few centuries brought the entire globe into a single magnetic field.

The United States was born by taking advantage of what Washington called the "occasional convulsions" of European politics, and from the beginning it has been a significant element in the process of European and world politics. The profound involvement of the United States in world affairs, even during the nineteenth century, was not a matter of choice, accident, or temperament. On the geostrategic map, the United States has been and remains a country of great importance, and it is as apparent today as in the time of Thucydides that "geography is destiny." The American colonies were pawns in the European wars of the seventeenth and eighteenth centuries. After the United States was established, it was universally recognized as a potential great power and then as a great power in fact. I might recall for you an episode illustrating this fact which took place not far from here. While the United States government was preoccupied with the Civil War, France and Austria, with the support of French troops, installed Maximilian as Emperor of Mexico. Immediately after Appomattox, while some hostilities were still going in the South, we sent General Sheridan and 50,000 hardened troopers to the Mexican border; then our diplomats in Paris and Washington expressed grave concern to the government of France. France decided that discretion was the better part of valor and withdrew, leaving Maximilian to his fate. It was considered so urgent to dispatch Sheridan to the Mexican border that he was denied permision to delay his departure for a few days in order to march up Pennsylvania Avenue in the Victory Parade.

If the United States is inevitably involved in world politics, either as participant or as victim, how shall we set about delineating the security problem the nation faces for the foreseeable future?

The place to begin answering that question is with the map of world politics—the famous map created by Mackinder and later developed by Spyckman and others, as it looks now, when planes and missiles can fly over the Arctic ice, submarines can navigate under it, and naval vessels are at risk, as the Falkland Islands conflict showed, as never before.

If one looks at the globe as a whole—and in defining American security, no lesser perspective is possible—9/12ths of its surface are occupied by the oceans and 2/12ths by what Madkinder called the "World Island"—Europe, Asia, and Africa, connected by land and backed by the Arctic circle, which in Mackinder's day was impregnable. Britain, Japan, and the Americas occupy 1/12th of the earth's surface and should be viewed as satellite islands off the coast of the vastly larger World Island. In 1919, when Mackinder published his most important book, 14/16ths of the world population lived on the World Island—the single continent of Europe, Asia, and Africa; 1/16th on Great Britain and Japan; and 1/16th on the American continent and the smaller islands. These proportions changed a little by 1978, the last year for which I have been able to find the relevant statistics. In that year, 13/16ths of the world population lived on the World Island, a drop of about 6 percent; the share of Great

Britain and Japan in world population fell about 2 1/2 percent to 0.6/16th in 1978; and the percentage of the world's population living in the Americas and the other islands rose 8.5 percent to 2.4/16ths.

What Mackinder called the Heartland of the World Island—the great central patch of Asia and Europe extending from the Arctic shores of Siberia to Persia and Baluchistan and from the Pacific coastal regions of Asia to the larger part of Germany—has until recently been inaccessible from the sea. As Catherine the Great once remarked during a period of diplomatic tension between Russia and Great Britain, "Let Pitt send his ships to Moscow." The Heartland area constitutes an enormous center of power from which military forces have attacked the coastal regions of Asia and Europe (the Rimlands, in Mackinder's terminology) since the beginning of time, and regions beyond the coasts as well. The moral of history is by no means a matter of merely antiquarian interest. The Soviet Union today is outflanking Norway, showing great interest in Iceland, and directly threatening Iran and Baluchistan; a brilliant American student of strategy once said Russia should never be allowed to go south of the line between Tehran and Kabul. Today the Soviet Union occupies Afghanistan and has forces in Indochina, putting pressure on China and Japan, and is devoting enormous efforts to its central goal, the separation of Europe from the United States and the neutralization of Europe and, therefore, of Japan and China as well, in consequence.

Those who have attempted to view history in this perspective have seemed to disagree about the relative importance of sea power and land power in the wars and diplomacy of the past. Equally, they seem to disagree today about the relative significance of air power and nuclear power as compared to the older forms of land and sea power. Some advocates of sea power have undoubtedly exaggerated the military value of blockades and of economic warfare more generally, just as the enthusiasts for air power and nuclear power have made excessive claims in their turn. Nonetheless, the main positions in the literature of strategy are easily reconciled. Sea power is of immense utility in enabling the Island and Rimland powers to prevent any one power from dominating the Heartland, and thus achieving domination. But the bases of sea power are sometimes vulnerable to attack from the land, as Singapore was captured in World War II. And to be significant, sea power must be amphibious; its purpose is not to control the fishes, but to project military power on land. The defeat of the Spanish Armada did not end Spain's thrust for dominance in Europe; Elizabeth I had to fight with allies on the Continent to achieve that end, as her successors did against different aspirants for hegemony in the time of Marlborough, Wellington, and the leaders of the Western alliances in both the World Wars of this century. Similarly, for all the immense importance of air power as an adjunct to land and sea operations, it has not become an independent dimension of warfare, while the principal function of nuclear weapons thus far has been political, in permitting or not permitting states to use conventional or unconventional nonnuclear weapons.

In modern world politics, given modern technology in transportation, communication, and war, the military potential of the Eurasian-African land mass is even more overwhelming than in the past, if it were brought under the control of a single power bent on conquest. Western and Central Europe have formidable military resources; Russia is stronger than ever before; and Central Asia is no longer the home only of nomad horsemen armed with spears or old rifles. China is modernizing, and Japan is, of course, extremely powerful.

For the United States, an island state like Britain and Japan, the first problem of national security is therefore to help prevent the emergence of a decisive aggregation of power either in Europe or in Asia. We fought in two World Wars during this century to keep Germany from achieving a position of dominance in Europe. For the same reason, the Western allies united in NATO are preventing the Soviet Union from attaining the same goal. It is this consideration which makes Central Europe such an important pivot in the geography of power, and the independence of Poland, Czechoslovakia, Hungary, Yugoslavia, Bulgaria, and Rumania, therefore, so important to the security of the West. In 1962, President Kennedy told the Soviet Union that there could be no peace between our peoples until the Soviet Union carried out the promise of free elections in Eastern Europe it made at Yalta and Potsdam. That judgment will remain valid indefinitely.

Our security interest in the Pacific Basin is exactly parallel. As President Nixon and Chou En-Lai declared in their Shanghai communique of 1972, the United States and China are agreed in opposing "any hegemonial power in Asia." Later, despite intense

Soviet pressure, Japan adhered to that declaration: a classic instance of Island and Rimland powers combining to deter the strongest land power of the day from gaining ascendancy. This was the strategic consideration for which we fought the Korean and Vietnam wars. It justifies our interest in the Philippines, Taiwan, the ASEAN states, and of course the island nations of the South Pacific.

The security of the United States, then, must be viewed on a worldwide scale. Our problems in maintaining that security are the same as those with which Great Britain had to deal over the centuries, first within the European region, and more recently throughout the world. While the NATO alliance holds firm, we do not have to be concerned with modern Germany as a candidate for dominance. The Soviet Union is playing that role in world politics at the moment. For the simplest of geopolitical reasons, we cannot allow one power to control the Soviet Union, Germany, and Central Europe, on the Atlantic side, or the Soviet Union, China, and Japan in the Pacific Basin.

If the United States conducts a calm, steady deterrent policy, the Soviet quest for hegemony will fail, as all such quests have failed since the heyday of the Roman Empire. The nations determined to protect or to restore their political independence and territorial integrity far outweigh the Soviet Union in political and military power. If those nations are well and prudently led, the Soviet Union should come before too long to see the folly—and the immense cost—of its imperial adventure.

The nuclear weapon and the state of the nuclear

balance give a special dimension to our task in maintaining the solidarity of the regional coalitions indispensable to our national security. The Soviet Union views nuclear weapons as primarily political in character, and we should do so as well. No one can promise that the world will be spared nuclear war, especially if irrational political leaders acquire nuclear weapons. But the Soviet Union is most unlikely to wage a nuclear war so long as the United States retains a credible capacity for nuclear retaliation. The Soviet Union is building its nuclear force to astronomic levels not to unleash nuclear war, but to separate the United States from its allies and associates in the Atlantic and the Pacific and to compel American neutrality while it gains control of the Eurasian land mass, Africa, and even the Caribbean through the use of conventional forces, proxies, terrorism, and propaganda. In the nuclear arms negotiations, the Soviet position has been clear. The Soviet negotiators have been using every weapon of propaganda and intimidation to persuade us and our European allies to accept a Soviet position of nuclear superiority. This is why they have pressed for the inclusion of British and French nuclear forces in the negotiation, although they know that those forces are no threat to the far superior Soviet arsenal, but exist for quite different national purposes. And they have held out so far for agreements based on the principle of equal reduction, not reduction to equal levels, which was the basis for the 1922 Washington naval agreements. The Soviet approach to the negotiations would make the crucial Soviet advantage in ground based ballistic missiles even bigger and more intimidating than it is now.

To accept the Soviet position in the nuclear arms negotiations—or indeed to compromise with it in any way—would make it impossible for us to protect our most fundamental national interest in world politics, that in achieving and preserving a stable balance of power. The Soviet Union has so far been seeking arms agreements incompatible with true detente— agreements which would compel us to withdraw from Europe and Asia, and return to a position of dependent neutrality in world affairs. President Reagan's greatest foreign policy success so far—and it is a major success—is that he has led the NATO allies and Japan to support our insistence in the Geneva negotiations that agreement be based on Soviet-American equality. The diplomacy of the nuclear arms negotiations has been complex and demanding. It has required not only intense bargaining with the Soviet representatives but frequent and anxiety ridden consultations with the NATO allies and Japan as well. Thus far, it has been altogether successful, as the Soviet Union has now recognized. The Allies have calmly overcome intense Soviet propaganda efforts and carried out the NATO two-track decision of 1979, made while President Carter was in office; that decision called for the deployment in Europe of modern American intermediate range ground based missiles unless the Soviet Union reached a satisfactory agreement on that class of weapons. The NATO two-track decision was not a wise basis for negotiations, since it invited maximum Soviet intransigence. But it would have been catastrophic for the allies to have changed their policy under Soviet propaganda pressure. The result was a major defensive victory for the Western alliance systems—a victory like the battle of the Marne in 1914, Gettysburg, Midway, or the Battle of Britain in 1940, a victory which makes other victories possible in the future.

When I refer to possible future victories in the muscular diplomatic struggle between the Soviet Union and the Western industrial democracies, I am not referring to the possibility of reaching agreements on the control of nuclear weapons and other weapons of mass destruction. Such agreements could be useful in the quest for peace if they are compatible with true detente, that is, if they do not deny the United States the capacity to reach and sustain deterrent equilibrium against Soviet aggression. They could be disastrous if they prevent us from maintaining the balance or serve to legitimize the Soviet program of indefinite expansion based on the aggressive use of nonnuclear forces. For arms control agreements are not a substitute for peace, or a magical device for achieving peace by a stroke of the pen. For nearly twenty-five years, we have done ourselves terrible injury by treating arms control agreements as if they were talismans of peace. The fever of self-deception in the West about the value of arms control has by no means run its course.

People often speak about the Cold War as if it were a distasteful Great Power Game, in which the behavior of the United States and the Soviet Union could be equated. This comforts some as a convenient excuse for self-righteously declaring "a pox on both your houses" and avoiding the responsibility of choice and action. But it profoundly mistakes the nature of Soviet policy and the role of law in the social process. The rules against aggression of the Charter of the United Nations are not empty formalities. They distill the lessons which the finest minds of our civilization have drawn from centuries of experience in the struggle to control the demonic plague of international war. The United States and the other industrial democracies respect those rules and are still abiding by them, although they cannot afford the luxury of that policy much longer. The Soviet Union is openly violating the law of the Charter both in open aggressions, like those in Cambodia and Afghanistan, and in its support of insurrection and terrorism from the Caribbean to South East Asia. The diplomacy of the Cold War is not a game. It is one facet of a politico-military contest conducted in the nuclear environment by methods which the nuclear balance makes not unreasonably imprudent. The most fundamental interest of the Western nations is in restoring the integrity of the rule against aggression and the stability of the state system, conceived as a loose association of independent and sovereign states. The goal of the Soviet program of expansion is something quite different—the ancient dream of imperial domination.

Whether we achieve future victories in this politico-military struggle depends entirely on the wisdom and spirit with which our affairs are conducted. Of all the revolutions which have transformed world politics in the last seventy years, the most important in my view is the revolution in the climate of opinion in the West. For I regard the decline of optimism, energy, and self-confidence throughout the West as the main source of the widespread Western anxiety and defeatism with regard to our future in the world community.

There is no objective basis for such pessimism. As Lord Carrington recently reminded us, the West has all the cards in its hand—a far superior economy; humane social systems; devoted populations; adequate military potential; and above all the cause of peace. We can, and in the nuclear world we must, insist on peace, true peace, as the goal of our foreign policy. The globe is smaller than it used to be, but it is still spherical; it is hard to imagine wars which can be allowed to rage unchecked without providing the Soviet Union opportunities for further expansion in areas of strategic consequence.

A great historian of the Roman Empire was once asked why Rome fell. "They lost their nerve," he replied. We should take his comment to heart.